A COLD-BLOODED BUSINESS

A COLD-BLOODED BUSINESS

*Adultery, Murder, and a Killer's Path from the
Bible Belt to the Boardroom*

MAREK FUCHS

SKYHORSE PUBLISHING

Skyhorse Publishing books may be purchased in bulk at special discounts for sales promotion, corporate gifts, fund-raising, or educational purposes. Special editions can also be created to specifications. For details, contact the Special Sales Department, Skyhorse Publishing, 555 Eighth Avenue, Suite 903, New York, NY 10018 or info@skyhorsepublishing.com.

www.skyhorsepublishing.com

10 9 8 7 6 5 4 3 2 1

Library of Congress Cataloging-in-Publication Data
Fuchs, Marek, 1967-
A cold-blooded business : Adultery, Murder, and a Killer's Path from the Bible Belt to the Boardroom / Marek Fuchs.
p. cm.
ISBN 978-1-60239-254-0 (alk. paper)
1. Murder--Kansas--Olathe. 2. Harmon, David, d. 1982. 3. Raisch, Melinda.
4. Mangelsdorf, Mark. I. Title.
HV6534.O42F83 2008
364.152'3092--dc22
2008013285

Printed in the United States of America

For Lori, Lyra, Emmett and Oliver, who put up with way too much, and with grace and warmth give back laughs and more than I could ever dream of in exchange.

CONTENTS

"And God is faithful; he will not let you be tempted beyond what you can bear. But when you are tempted, he will also provide a way out so that you can stand up under it."

—1 Corinthians 10:13

FOREWORD

She asked me if I had seen the article; I had. While drinking our respective morning coffees, my editor at the *New York Times* and I had both happened upon a small mention in a local paper. It wasn't much, several hundred words of simple facts, and not too many at that. A man who lived on a choice street in Pelham, New York—an upscale suburb of New York City—had just been implicated in an old Kansas murder. With the help of a female accomplice, he was thought to have killed a sleeping man. Quite brutally, it seemed.

On any ordinary day, there might be legal and ethical lapses among the well-heeled residents of Pelham, but little in the way of murder, much less wholesale slaughter. This was intriguing. Had a murderer, undetected for two decades, lived in close quarters with CEOs, investment bankers, and venture capitalists? Was he one of them? One of those people with an innate and expedient ability to succeed in our world? Probably. The article mentioned that the accused's attorney was Michael "Mickey" Sherman, who had represented Kennedy family member Michael Skakel in that cold murder case. Sherman had clout and did not come cheap.

Life's path is always fraught with lurches and surprise, but this journey from Kansas to Pelham and the height of New York respectability seemed like an especially crooked line. And then there was the name of the town back in Kansas: Olathe. I wasn't even sure how to pronounce it, but for some odd reason, it looked familiar. A trip to my bookshelf told me why. Truman Capote's *In Cold Blood* had profiled the pair of murderers who'd used Olathe as their base, departing from the small east Kansas town to kill the Clutter family and returning there later that same blood-soaked, wakeful night. This murder, though, was already different. In *In Cold Blood*, the pair of murderers had stumbled from crime to crime and were caught a month and a half after the murder, eventually executed together. No such tidy, frontier moral play here. This Pelham man and his female cohort, who were originally suspects but somehow went free, had gone their separate ways and apparently had been living accomplished lives in the two decades since their own particular blood-soaked, wakeful night. Were they weighed down by remorse? Or were they able to put a tight lid on the guilt? Perhaps they were totally innocent, wrongfully accused. Even the authorities must have some doubts. The woman had been indicted for murder, but the man was only named as a co-conspirator, as yet not formally charged. Why not adhere to the more common practice of formally indicting both suspects?

There seemed to be far more questions than answers.

My editor—the incomparable Jeanne Pinder—gave me the go-ahead. Without further delay, I was off to Kansas.

PROLOGUE

God has failed too many on this one, thought Detective Bill Wall as he ambled, soaking wet, toward the large home with the brick façade. It was warm for an Ohio December, and the temperature meant that rain, not snow, fell from the slate-gray sky—and that was no advantage. In a bit of poor planning, Wall and his companion, Detective Steve James, had forgotten their umbrellas. Their footsteps splashed against the steps of the house belonging to Melinda Raisch, formerly known as Melinda Harmon.

They were there to investigate the unsolved murder of Melinda's first husband, David Harmon. For almost twenty years, the case had been famously unsolved in their home state of Kansas, but Wall had a hunch this case could be wrapped up with just a turn of that front doorknob.

The players in the crime were memorialized in the depths of the collective unconscious back in Olathe: a pretty newlywed, Melinda Lambert, the one all the boys desired for her pert, all-American looks and her bright, eager eyes; a young, handsome college student, Mark Mangelsdorf, student body president and one of the most popular guys on campus; and David Harmon, Melinda's adoring, twenty-five-year-old husband, who one dark winter evening in 1982 was bludgeoned to death in his own bed. It was a slaying so gruesome that the first responders on the scene thought the victim had been shot in the face point blank with a shotgun.

A dozen blows had fallen on David's sleeping face, when probably three would have served to kill. His face had been rendered featureless. One eyeball was dislodged and had rolled onto the floor. His nose and cheekbones were utterly destroyed. His jaw was cracked in several places, and the killer had been in such a fervid state that he had, in his haste, delivered an errant shot to David's neck, crushing it. Pieces of David's brain had sprayed about the bedroom.

David's wife Melinda and her friend Mark Mangelsdorf were the prime suspects. The brutal murder sparked dissent and division within the town: between the relatively newly arrived Church of the Nazarene, an evangelical Christian denomination of which Melinda, David, and Mark were members, and the long-established Olathe residents. Because of the church's unusual actions after the murder, many thought it was protecting its flock, even at the risk of harboring criminals. Some thought the entire case against Mark and Melinda was character assassination and that the unsubstantiated rumors of a "Nazarene divorce" stemmed from fear of the town's growing population of evangelicals.

Evangelicals stood in animus against farm families and their more measured attachment to Jesus. Neighbor set upon neighbor, with the naturally deferential manners of the Midwest all but lost, as if to prairie fire.

Even the vaunted Kansas Bureau of Investigation had failed to prove the identity of the murderer or murderers. No one had spent even one moment in jail for David's murder.

And yet, the two prime suspects had a story that was so flimsy, it amounted to a whispered taunt: "Catch me if you can." Now, approaching Melinda Raisch's front door two decades later, Detective Wall thought the duo should have been rotting in prison all those years, not enjoying charmed lives in their respective high societies. But here Wall and James were, wading out of the investigation's still waters. What would happen now? The investigators who had come before them—stymied by a dearth of conclusive evidence—had at one point become so desperate for clues that they had resorted to consulting a fortune teller. Did Wall and James face similar failure?

A third man was along for the ride, an Ohio detective named Eric Griffin, a local chaperone who had done some reconnaissance of the place to make sure Melinda would be alone, without children, without her successful cosmetic-dentist husband, and, most of all, without her father, an old man now who—they were not surprised to learn—lived nearby and might still be ready to proffer advice and stand nose to nose with police to protect his child, as he had done back in 1982.

Griffin was there to make sure the Kansas boys did not misuse their authority and, as tempting as it was, perform a bit of rough frontier justice. He'd let them give the rich lady a workaround, though they would pretty much have to conform to state law. He was the supervisor as long as they were in his jurisdiction. He was also there to radio for backup, in the unlikely event that this visit to a suburban mom took a dark turn.

Through the large windows of the Raisch's stately home shone the lights of two brilliantly appointed Christmas trees. "Looks like Nordstrom's," Wall said to James, echoing what they viewed as the theme of this case—evil masquerading as normalcy.

It was a prime year for evil masquerading as normalcy. Just three months prior to the Ohio trip, nineteen hijackers had strolled onto four separate jet planes and in a single morning changed the face of modern history. It was now late December of 2001 and Wall and James, traveling through airports in the wake of September 11 with their guns in tow, had caused high drama, even with their badges, identification, and pale Kansan faces. Every aspect of this case seemed a lost cause, but coming from the town of Olathe, which, in the time since the murder had seen its open fields of wheat and wildflowers give way to suburban sprawl, Wall and James were used to demonstrating resilience in the face of change.

They anticipated that Melinda would be as unreceptive as she had been in 1982, when a group of high-placed evangelicals from the Church of the Nazarene cloaked her in a mantle of spiritual immunity. She was allowed to leave the city without being subjected to so much as a single formal police interview. Today, the plan was to mollify her, to make it seem as if she was not a suspect. At the same time, they would imply that they had new DNA evidence, which, depending on test results they hadn't received yet, might or might not be true. They would flap their gums like forensic specialists in the hope that she watched too many real crime shows and would fold.

They would also threaten to blab around town about the crime.

Her husband—the new one—was a well-to-do cosmetic dentist, and the pair gave heartily to local charitable organizations. The detectives would tell a few key neighbors, clients of the dental practice, fellow church members, and even the recipients of Melinda's charitable donations if it'd help seal the deal.

Of course, it was all a bluff. If she told them to get lost or, more likely, "No, thank you," or "I have to speak to an attorney," they would stop themselves from calling her some choice names, then depart and head back to Kansas, fingers crossed that on their way home *they* weren't arrested at the airport.

At the very least, in just catching a glimpse of Melinda in the doorway, they could take a quick measure. Her looks were an avenue of intrigue. She had been so alluring back in 1982. Had guilt exacted a toll upon that attractive face, that inviting body? From the look of her home—and current photos of Mark, her suspected partner in the bloodbath who had not aged a lick—they highly doubted it.

As the detectives reached the threshold, they affected flat gazes. James would play the sympathetic cop, Wall the more aggressive one.

In the end, it wasn't a knock on the door, or a forceful twist of the doorknob, but a doorbell that announced their presence. Local detective Eric Griffin had done the honors.

The door opened and there was a moment's pause all around. Melinda stood in her ornate foyer, glowing in the Christmas lights, dressed in nothing but a robe with a towel wrapped tight around her hair.

She then did something neither Wall nor James had expected during the hours they had stared bleary-eyed and hunched over that case file in the old-fashioned Olathe police station. Before they had even identified themselves, she beckoned the detectives inside.

PART ONE

"The good man brings good things out of the good stored up in him,
and the evil man brings evil things out of the evil stored up in him."

—Matthew 12:35

ONE

David Harmon was a product of Chili, pronounced with long "i"s—CHI-lye—a downtrodden cow town in upstate New York off the Erie Canal Expressway, a highway in name only. The town's forefathers appeared to have chosen both the name and its pronunciation on a whim. An old timer will say the name may be the same as the bean dish, before letting a smile creep up one side of his mouth: "But we pronounce it right."

Sitting unnoticed along the way from Syracuse to Buffalo, near Rochester, Chili was always a modest place, even for a rural outpost whose northernmost regions once served as a stop along the Underground Railroad. Its winters are bleak, with billows of Canadian snow. Farming is a stubborn act of survival, with depth-charge temperatures in January and February and crop-killing frosts in spring.

Chili has been home to generations of Harmons, whose lives centered largely around prayer and farming. Like most Chili residents, they were known for a remoteness and stoicism, even when the "big stuffs," as government officials were called, annexed the family homestead to expand the local airport. There were howls of local protest, though little from the Harmons themselves. Were it not for the confiscation of the farm, young John Harmon (David's father) would have been land-rich by inheritance. Then again, tilling the land was a lifelong commitment. And even if farming were performed with diligence, the backbreaking labor would not have produced more than a modest livelihood; and that's if the weather held. Which it might not—no matter how often or hard he prayed.

* * * *

The Harmon family settled in Chili in 1838, and John, who remained long after the others had moved away or gone to glory, was born there during the Great Depression. Bred into John were all the proper Christian convictions about how we live in a created order. He was reticent by nature and upbringing, and born into a family whose routine was work, pray, sleep, and fish. His father, without the family farm to tend, became an engineer.

When the time came for John to choose a college, he went to Roberts Wesleyan College in North Chili. Wesleyan is a Christian school founded by Benjamin Titus Roberts, a lawyer turned missionary. For some of his more liberal stands on slavery and women's rights, Roberts had been kicked out by the faithful of the Methodist Episcopal Church, but landed as a bishop with the Free Methodists. He started the school as Chili Seminary in 1866, and while the college changed name and location several times over the years, its overall approach of educating under the eyes of God remained the same. At Roberts, John felt in place and at peace.

John got his masters degree in education at the secular University of Rochester and chose to teach elementary school, drawn to both the security he felt the job offered and the meaningfulness he felt it imparted. Working with children was ideal for John, since he was socially strained with adults.

He married Sue, the first girl he met in college. From the outset of their marriage, a slight hint of irreverence, even wickedness, in Sue always brought a quick—if sometimes embarrassed—smile to John's face. Once, while hiking up a mountain with their dear friends, the DeHavens, John passed wind at an unintentionally loud volume.

"Geez Louise, John," Sue piped up, "that's the most you've spoken all day."

The two were Nazarene Christians. The Church of the Nazarene is a Protestant church in the Wesleyan-Holiness tradition, tracing its roots to 1908. It was founded to spread the message of "scriptural holiness," or "Christ-like living," throughout the world. Nazarenes believe in a higher purpose in life through victory over sin, in evangelism, in a strict interpretation of the Bible, in preaching the gospel to the poor, and, most of all, in salvation, or "perfection," through a personal relationship with God through Jesus Christ.

Though Sue and John considered themselves saved, they didn't believe themselves invulnerable. The two assumptions they allowed were that life was not ruled by chance, and that all souls can be saved from even our darkest sins.

The couple had one child. David Harmon was born on a windy day of malicious cold on January 3, 1957. He grew into a big, tall, handsome, dark-haired boy who was doted on by his parents. David grew up playing in his modest backyard, without the freedom or the burden of ancestral fields. Artistic, but with a linear mind, he made a hobby of sketching buildings. He dreamed of a professional life in architecture, or in engineering like his grandfather—but his real passions were sports and Jesus.

David played hockey both indoors and, given the frozen tundra that was the Chili landscape, outdoors on ponds that froze up most of the winter. In high school, David would have liked to play varsity football. With his size, the football coach had his eye on him, but David had a trick knee that prevented him from playing. Instead, David devoted himself to pick-up sports and competitive Bible study.

David competed on a Bible Study Quiz team, where teams of five contestants raced to be the first to the buzzer with the correct answer. He studied for the competitions for hours every day. Even though the game had been a second choice to football, David never did anything in a detached way, and his team won the state championship.

When David was fifteen, he met a girl, Melinda Lambert, at Brooktondale Church Camp, a Nazarene summer camp outside Ithaca, New York. Melinda was the youngest child in her family, but with her older sister eleven years her senior, hers was not a "secondborn" childhood. She grew up in Syracuse like an only child in a doctrinaire household.

Her father, Dr. J. Wilmer (William) Lambert was a top Nazarene Church official, essentially an archbishop of the region including New York. Due to his prominence, Melinda was looked upon as the princess of the Nazarene Church, which certainly helped her social standing at camp.

Melinda could be controlling and rule-bound. At Brooktondale Church Camp, she alerted supervisors to the names and actions of boys and girls she found in compromising situations. Once, when she happened upon a group of teenagers throwing sticks and stones at a skunk to try to scare him into the Tabernacle, Melinda told a supervisor. In fact, telling on others was common at Bible camp, a practical function of the rules under God. Forbearance was essential.

Ironically, Melinda also came off as a flirt and a tease. Blonde and quick with a smile and a touch on your arm while talking or even while listening—which she always did with appreciative laughter—Melinda was a stunner. She was talkative—maybe even too talkative—but if you were a boy, and you wanted her attention, it paid to listen to her.

Melinda did not have an overly purposeful mindset, and one was not required of her. Nor did she do particularly well in school. She was, however, broadly ambitious—for a suitable boy, a good marriage prospect and all that union might bring home to her.

God, she was always told, has a way of making a way for you.

Bible camp was a complicated place for a pubescent teenager. Dating in this conservative environment, where there could be no public displays of affection and very little privacy was allowed, was no easy trick. They were teenagers in the 1970s, but in no way part of that era. Luckily, everything about Melinda—including her sexuality and her ambition— was made less sinful by the absoluteness of her faith. She was overt in her declarations of spirituality, and absolute in her observance of her church's prescriptions. She was excited about camp, God, and boys—specifically an agreeable and somewhat pliable one named David Harmon.

Melinda pursued David throughout her time at the camp. Whenever possible, she sat next to him in the Tabernacle, cuddled up close, and laughed at all his jokes. David was prominent because of his Bible Quiz accomplishments, his size—he was 6'3"—and his good looks. He was clearly going places, which was more than you could say for the many less impressive boys who spent the summer with their noses buried in the Bible. And who, after all, could land Melinda if not David? Smart and athletic without being cocky, David was also witty and fun. He loved a well-executed practical joke.

One year at Bible camp, he and Chad DeHaven—three years older than David and a friend from Chili who acted like a de facto older brother—drove a Volkswagen to the altar of the camp's Tabernacle. Turning the car off before the Tabernacle filled with fumes, David and DeHaven affixed a sign to the rear bumper, facing the pews, that read, "Shhhh. I'm praying." They ran back to the bunk and waited for the surprise at Sunday morning services.

Almost immediately after camp ended, David and Melinda began a long-distance relationship. The two wanted to see each other nearly every weekend, so with David in Chili and Melinda two hours away in Syracuse, their parents stepped in to help. Often, the Harmons drove David to meet the Lamberts halfway. Almost always, David went home with the Lamberts. Melinda's family was impressed with David. He was humble, religiously observant, and gentle with their daughter. They welcomed without hesitation this inherently decent young man.

When summer returned, David and Melinda went back to camp, drawn both to each other and to the feeling of acceptance the camp offered them. Inspiration and public displays of spirituality—such as carrying around Bibles, praying openly, and talking about God and faith—were expected and prized among that generation of evangelicals. At camp, David always had in hand a guide book to soul-winning, which, as the second sentence of its Foreword put it, is *not* soul-scalping. *The Church of Winning Souls: A Handbook for Personal Evangelism in the Local Church,* by V. H. Lewis, was less than a hundred pages, but in that space was a complete, albeit somewhat repetitive, guide to being a good evangelical Nazarene.

"Evangelicalism," wrote Lewis, "must be our method of advance as a church. We offer neither ritual nor ceremony as a substitute for salvation. Souls can know Christ as a personal Savior in a personal experience, through evangelicalism. We must not and shall not fail to evangelize! Our church was brought into being through the fires of evangelicalism. May its flame burn high on the altars of our church!"

Later, Lewis wrote, "When the church loses its fervor and drifts in a parallel course with the world, the Holy Spirit withdraws."

Mr. Lewis, David soon learned, was one of many of Melinda's cousins who were highly placed within the church. But David was most intrigued by Melinda's father, Dr. Lambert, who was aggressive and worldly in a way his own father was not. Lambert had an air of quiet superiority and a reputation for being demanding, tight-fisted, judgmental; he also took good care of relatives by finding them work in and around the church, as well as housing them, accumulating properties as he went along.

David graduated high school in 1975, earning a National Merit Scholarship among many other awards. His future was a wide-open road. He and Melinda began taking classes at Olivet Nazarene University in the fall. Nazarene teens commonly paired off and married by the age of twenty, and David and Melinda were no exception.

The wedding was beautifully arranged; David and his wedding party looked ascendant in their powder-blue tuxes and yellow corsages. It was all as innocent and perfect as any parents—especially fastidiously religious ones—could hope for.

It was no surprise that David and Melinda left Chili shortly after they were married. David would not follow his own father out into the world, but rather Melinda's. Dr. Lambert had just received a promotion in the church hierarchy, rising to become the general superintendent of Zone Two, as it was known in church parlance. The Nazarene headquarters in Kansas City was thriving, and Lambert would soon become its central figure.

Nazarenes were migrating in droves to Kansas, where development was replacing farming, and new opportunities abounded. Kansas seemed like the right place for David and Melinda to begin the next stage of their lives. David could finish his degree at the University of Kansas. Melinda could easily put the secretarial degree she received at Olivet to good use. The decision was a natural one.

God was making a way for Melinda and David Harmon.

Two

When Dick Hickock and Perry Smith killed four members of the Clutter family in the western reaches of Kansas in 1959, the pair chose Olathe (pronounced oh-LAY-thuh) as their staging ground. The two career chiselers, who had met in the penitentiary, set out from Olathe the day of the murders and, afterward, late that night, melted right back into town, all but unnoticed. The murders unsettled Kansas and the farm states surrounding it like little before. For weeks the Clutters' murderers could not be found. But frightful as it was, Hickock and Smith's run of freedom was brief and unproductive, involving nothing more than six weeks of petty crime and fizzled murder plots. The larcenous buddies had become killers when they took the lives of the Clutters, but—and there was at least comfort to be had in this—they never killed again. Hickock and Perry were hanged in the early 1960s at the Kansas state prison in Lansing and, were it not for Truman Capote, who documented their crime in the pages of *In Cold Blood*, that would have been the end of that.

Since the 1850s, when the Kansas School for the Deaf opened in Olathe, the town had stood home to an unlikely mix of farmers and deaf-mutes. Families tilled the flat land that had been handed down through the generations. The people were churchgoing folk. The more affluent ones—which was not to say wealthy—were those who had dairy farms in addition to wheat fields. In the evenings, the farmers and their families went into town to walk, which meant around the courthouse square. Girls married the boys they had grown up with and, if their husbands happened to die, say, in a farming accident, they married other boys they had grown up with.

The Church of the Nazarene came to Olathe in 1930, when it was chartered with twenty members. Things were put together with string and wax at first; for years, revival services were held in various spaces, including a creamery, an abandoned church, and a munitions depot. The latter was famous locally for its swayback roof.

The Reverend C. J. Garrett, who migrated from Ottawa, was the church's first pastor, and his sermon topics, reported in the local paper, were all variations on a single theme (subjects from "A Trip Through Hell" to "Is Olathe Hell?"). His flock grew exponentially.

The pivotal moment for the church came in the 1950s when the national Church of the Nazarene decided that God wanted them to open up their world headquarters just one-half hour from Olathe, across the border in Kansas City, Missouri, to "make disciples of all nations" (Matthew 28:19).

The arrival of the world headquarters ushered in a period of migration of Nazarene Christians to "little Olathe," as Truman Capote called it. Olathe was becoming a hub for the church.

A coterie of mostly professional Evangelical Christians—including the Lamberts—was becoming a vital force in reshaping this part of

Kansas, bringing with them not only the church, but all the businesses, politics, and concerns that accompanied the church. This was not the high-wheat plains of western Kansas, but east, closer to Kansas City, Missouri, where suburbs were replacing farmland.

The people of Olathe weren't hankering for any big changes. The big cities—Kansas City and, farther afield, the industrial bastion of Wichita—were for the middlemen with pickup trucks piled high with corn, the occasional day tripper, or the unlucky farmers who were reduced to seeking city work.

So the demographic shift—some might say lurch—that was transforming Olathe, Kansas, did not sit easy with the old timers. These newcomers—who came to the frontier a century or two after the initial heavy lifting was finished—were religious to a standard that unsettled even the locals, who responded, in their old-line prairie twang, "Those ones have all come down with a bad case of religion."

Located in the middle of Johnson County and close to the geographic center of the United States, Olathe (the Shawnee word for "beautiful") began to be known as the buckle of the East Kansas Bible Belt.

Olathe's four-thousand-seat church, called College Church of the Nazarene, was built in 1968 to "bring God's love to a dying world" (as the church's promotional materials noted with considerable pride). Its steeple stretches upward as the sharpest and most prominent feature between earth and heaven for miles around. It remains the local skyline's most identifiable structure. When the sky is awash in Kansas reds during a particularly beguiling sunset, the steeple appears as a welcoming symbol of solace and comfort. When a storm or tornado approaches, it can appear imposing.

In 1968, the General Assembly of the Nazarene Church chose Olathe as the location for its college after Bob Osborne, the president of Patron's State Bank & Trust, pledged the land on which it was built. The college, today known as MidAmerica Nazarene University, or MNU, was centered around Christ in general, but organized, from its creation, around the Church of the Nazarene in particular.

The college, originally called MidAmerica Nazarene College, opened its doors as a Christian liberal arts college with 263 students. The wild hairdos, frock coats, and casual morality popular elsewhere were not found here. Students were not allowed to drink alcohol, play cards, dance, or watch movies, among many other prohibitions up to—and obviously including—premarital sex. While professors did double duty as movie "sentries," standing watch at the local movie houses over the weekends to make sure no MNC students entered, those looking for drink or cinema could drive an hour in either direction outside of Olathe. Those craving intimacy merely needed to drive to the first remote Olathe street they could find (the police still joke about parked cars with steamed windows from the heat of Bible college students).

Students at MNC were required to attend church twice a week— though most went even more frequently—to bear testament to Jesus, and to encourage others to save their own souls. The church technically sat just outside the school's boundaries but, for practical purposes, it was the center of campus.

Guiding principles at MNC were the ideas of being faithful to Jesus, spreading God's word, and striving for "heart purity," or holiness. The result was, quite literally, an attempt at perfection—an attempt to live up to the same standards that Jesus did. This is a lofty goal but one the Nazarenes believed to be attainable. Therefore, fighting imperfection or evil was crucial at MNC.

The search for perfection had its casualties, however regrettable. But good evangelical Christians did not come ready-made. As time progressed, MNC produced good Christians in increasingly large numbers, and today the university's student body is two thousand members strong. In the church parking lot on Sundays you can spot bumper stickers announcing, "Jesus Loves All, But He Likes Me Most."

* * * *

"Me" could very easily refer to Mark Mangelsdorf. Mangelsdorf was one of the newcomers thronging to this part of Kansas. In fact, Mark stood out among the new arrivals at MNC. Big-bodied, at 6'4", and hard-working, Mark was smart and ambitious, with a fervent belief that he would be rewarded for his toil.

Mark was born in 1960 in St. Louis, the middle child sandwiched between his older brother, Ray Jr., and his younger sister, Patricia. His father, Ray, had grown up Catholic but allowed his wife, Mickie, to raise their children as evangelicals in the Christian & Missionary Alliance (C&MA), a denomination closely aligned with the Nazarenes.

The C&MA Church is less literal about the Bible than the Nazarenes. Founded by Albert Benjamin Simpson around the turn of the twentieth century, its two major tenets are that: 1) members should donate their worldly riches to support foreign missionary work, and 2) for the highly observant, their exercise of faith would bring physical healing. (The latter belief was influenced by Exodus 15:26: "He said, 'If you listen carefully to the voice of the Lord your God and do what is right in his eyes, if you pay attention to his commands and keep all his decrees, I will not bring on you any of the diseases I brought on the Egyptians, for I am the Lord, who heals you.'")

Mickie did not stay with the C&MA for long. The family lived in St. Louis's Hazelwood section, a lower-middle-class area with few professionals, and she was drawn to the more ascetic and literal Nazarene Church, whose doctrine required more supplication and forbade the usual drinking, smoking, dancing, card playing, and most of the other favorite pastimes in her neighborhood. For Mickie, the Bible was more than metaphor; it was a blueprint for living. She was attracted to the Nazarene traditionalism and social teaching, combined with that chance at salvation through self improvement and perfecting one's soul.

Ray Sr.'s job at Reynolds Metal (where Reynolds Wrap is made) didn't pay enough to send three children to parochial school, so the brothers worked as night custodians for the church in exchange for tuition. Reverend Wayne Moss, their teacher and youth pastor, said that in all his years of Christian education he never saw students work harder for their education than did the Mangelsdorfs.

The two boys shared a work ethic but little else. Ray had been a fat little kid—75 pounds at the age of three, 120 pounds by the first grade. Mark had been luckier weight-wise, tall but never fat. Mark—studious and well-behaved—was the family's golden boy. He would often bake with his mother, specializing in cookies for church bake sales. In contrast, Ray was rebellious, a boy who might be headed in the wrong direction. Mark and Ray could not interact without fighting.

The Nazarene Church initially galvanized Ray, but any change for the better didn't last long. As a teenager, Ray smoked, drank, and fought with other boys, and sometimes his father tried to set him straight, but the corporal punishment he meted out did not seem to take.

As for Mark, he was a master of detail, unstinting in his ambition to please his teachers. Mark was a pragmatist. He went about things, even as a boy, systematically. His speech was clipped and precise. He was efficient and diplomatic. You might surmise he would become the ultimate corporate operator. That he was capable of fury seemed inconceivable.

After Mark graduated from high school, he joined the others migrating to Olathe to enroll in MNC in 1978. His brother enrolled the same year, having taken a year off after high school.

David Penrose, a friend from childhood, planned to get a seminary degree, which is why he, like many in the Hazelwood section who attended the Nazarene Church school and summer camp, also went to MNC. Penrose shifted gears on his way to studying for the pulpit, becoming a behavioral psychologist for the criminally insane.

"In church and school," said Penrose, "we were always taught to avoid any appearance of evil."

"Mark," said David, "knew everything about avoiding the appearance of evil. He knew how to be the model citizen." Unlike his brother Ray, who cavorted with girls, Mark dutifully withheld. Girls—and all the sin and temptation they involved—would simply have to wait.

"He learned to overcome teenage libido," Penrose said.

"But," Penrose added, "try to modulate every impurity at any one point in your life, and you might run the risk of temporarily distorting your soul."

Mark's soul was consumed with the quest for perfectionism. By the time he attended MNC, he had gravitated toward business, and he seemed to thrive in the constrained environment of the college. His freshman year he was the epitome of pious. At the dorm's nightly bed check he was always in bed on time and alone. He was skillful and public in his spirituality: He would talk of his love for Jesus, proselytize, and maintain strict conformity with the rules of the college and of the church. Such behavior was expected at a Bible college, but Mark's version came without sanctimony. He was just plain friendly, even in passing conversation, with the observant and nonobservant alike.

Mark's brother Ray, however, remained unconvinced of the sanctity of the Nazarene approach and ultimately succumbed to the old temptations. Part of his doubt stemmed from a comparative religion class he was taking. In this class he heard for the first time the voices of other religions and found in them some validity. The "holiness" movement did not always seem so holy to Ray.

Soon he had a pet tarantula named Fuzz Butt in his dorm room. After installing the spider, he began to party, smoke marijuana, play football, bed women, and get into the occasional squabble or fistfight. During one night of carousing, he beat up a classmate in his car and left him by the roadside. Eventually, Ray dropped out of the college. He clearly didn't fit in on a campus where freshmen still wore beanies and Nazarene college boys associated with girls through a practice called "parloring." As immortalized in their 1982 yearbook: "Freshman girls eagerly await the ring of the hall phone and the sound of a nervous male voice asking to see them in the parlor. With fluttering heart and clammy hands, she meets her suitor and they proceed to play Uno, order a pizza, study together, or just talk."

The Mangelsdorf brothers, despite the same upbringing, seemed almost unrelated. In Mark's junior year, he was elected Sergeant-at-Arms, or attorney general, of the student body. Then, in 1981, as Mark was entering his senior year, he was elected student body president, or "Head Fred," as the position was called in jest.

Even in the restrained atmosphere of MNC, Mark thought you could be spiritual without being brooding or repressed. By his senior year, Mark had staged six Christian rock concerts on campus.

A review of one of his concerts ran under the school newspaper headline CHRIST GLORIFIED. The review began, "What do you think makes a successful Christian singing group? Is it good instruments and equipment, talent, a great back-up or making a lot of money? I believe that it is none of these things. Unlike a secular group, whose success is marked by how much money they make per concert or how many gold albums they have, I believe a Christian group's success can be measured in one thing: how much they glorify Christ. If Farrell and

Farrell [the band's name] were to be compared to how close to that goal they came, they would hit the center of the target."

Mark also helped put together the most successful revival week—the campus week of prayer and togetherness—that MNC had seen in its limited history.

Three

Newlyweds Melinda and David arrived in Olathe in 1977, making a home in one of the several residences that Melinda's father owned—a duplex with a downstairs living room and an upstairs bedroom, decent sized but not quite big enough for a family.

Their home was typical of the type that was popping up all over town. A nod to the surge in construction brought on by those coming to build their lives around the college, the recent local joke was that Olathe wasn't the Shawnee Indian word for "beautiful," but rather for "duplex."

Still, Olathe retained some unique characteristics, which took some getting used to. Dozens of trains came through the town each day. Twenty-three railroad crossings effectively bisected the town. With trains sounding their whistles as they approached each crossing arm, daily life in Olathe was a series of interruptions, when conversation and work halted until the whistle abated, only to resume until the next train whistle blew. Driving in Olathe was likewise an exercise in patience. Going anywhere often involved waiting at railroad crossings as a long freight train passed.

David enrolled at nearby University of Kansas to complete his degree, switching his focus from engineering and architecture to business administration. Melinda's father procured for her a job as a secretary at the Nazarene headquarters in Kansas City.

Dr. Lambert also set David up with a job at Patron's Bank. Patron's was on Santa Fe Avenue, the main thoroughfare through the town and once part of the overland trade route to Mexico called the Sante Fe Trail. David was hired as an entry-level loan officer making around $13,000 a year.

Melinda's first job, for some reason—no one can remember why precisely—did not pan out. She was competent enough, but, as a former employee put it, maybe a touch too easily distracted, a touch too giggly when she joked.

Then her father got her a job with a well-regarded dean at MNC named Jim Smith, a real up-and-comer in church circles. Melinda was the perfect fit for the position. The work was regular without being overly demanding. Melinda kept the dean's schedule, typed his letters, and handled the convoy of matters going through the Student Life office. Had the Nazarene college job proved an ill fit, finding another job wouldn't have been a problem for her. Dr. Lambert was a successful and well-connected man with a stable of business interests, including apartment rentals that David oversaw as sideline work.

Not that Melinda was a career girl. An MNC yearbook photo of her at work ran with the caption: MELINDA HARMON FINDS SOMETHING TO SMILE ABOUT: FRIDAY. A career was not what her father wanted for her anyway. She would only work until she began to produce and raise good evangelicals. Unbeknownst to her father, though, Melinda and David kept condoms hidden away in David's night table. Using birth control was against church teachings, but considering their youth, the challenging economic times in Kansas circa 1980, and how observant the Harmons were in all other ways, perhaps the parenting path could wait a while.

Life on a college campus suited Melinda's flirtatious personality. Being part of the Student Life office allowed her limitless opportunities to meet new people, including the organizer of the campus's wildly popular Christian rock concerts, a strapping underclassman named Mark Mangelsdorf.

Mark always seemed to be going somewhere. And that somewhere often included a stopover at the office of the Dean of Student Life and, more specifically, at Melinda's desk. First, it was the concerts. All the arrangements ran through the Student Life office. Mark was also active as a resident assistant, one of the students appointed to supervise a floor of a dormitory to act as the administration's eyes and ears. This was a job of particular responsibility at MNC, given the regulations about opposite-sex visits, alcohol, movies, loose talk, card-playing, and other hedonistic transgressions.

Mark was poised and ambitious, like Melinda's father. He was not out to impress, but he did. No one breathed success on campus like Mark. He did not, as friends soon began to say of David, need just a little more time to find his adult bearings. Before too long, Melinda introduced Mark to David and the three became friends.

David's own work at the bank was not inspiring. He did impeccable work when the situation called for it, but that his heart was not in banking was soon apparent. He loved the floor hockey and racquetball he played (now joined by Mark), the youth groups he ran, and the charity work he did for the church. He taught Sunday School classes and organized Bible readings and sports for children. David also spent time with the author of the book he had so often carried around as a younger man—V. H. Lewis, who lived in Olathe. Lewis became like a second father to David.

Quietly, David still sketched buildings—grand ones and even small improvements to the existing ones he saw around him. He was busy, but he lacked the focused ambition of his past. "I'm a modest man," he once confided to a co-worker, before letting that droll Chili smile creep up half his face, "with a lot to be modest about."

With a slight air of helplessness, and a core of such obvious decency, David became the center of attention of a small circle of older women at work. David would show the women lists of gifts he intended to buy for Melinda, everything from jewelry to clothes. They were charmed by his dedication to Melinda, and his refusal to let reality intrude when they asked him how he planned to afford all these items. He would merely shrug in response. Despite the need for a higher gift allowance in his budget, some of the Patron's Gals, as they called themselves, assumed David would eventually leave banking to become a preacher. Others thought his modesty would hold him back; few preachers possessed that quality.

Patron's was a microcosm of the tension existing in Olathe at large. There was animosity between longtime bank employees who had arrived years before and those new ones who seemed to catapult over them for promotions (and who just happened to be connected with the Nazarene church). David, still in his early twenties, seemed more interested in playing practical jokes on his co-workers than climbing the corporate ladder at the bank. This seemed an unusual attitude for someone who longed to buy his wife pricey objects. Almost singular in his ability to bridge the various political worlds at the bank—perhaps because he had no desperate desire to accumulate power—he specialized in crawling across the carpeted floor, commando style, to shoot rubber bands at the ankles of the teller working the drive-through. Drivers were unaware that the teller was trying not to fall to pieces laughing. David also threw pencils in the air until they stuck in the ceiling tiles, only to watch them fall one by one as the teller dealt with the drive-through customers. Joy Hempy, the office receptionist and a frequent victim of his pranks, called David the "life blood of the office."

David was responsible, mostly professional, and easy to get along with; that, everyone who worked with him agreed on. Mark seemed eager to get along with him, too. The two regularly played floor hockey, though Mark was by far the better player. By this point David was getting on in pounds, up past 250, and mainly played goalie, where he nearly filled up the goal. It took him some time to find the necessary lefty goalie mitt, a rarity, but it served him well. The friendship of these two overgrown boys blossomed, and soon Mark was some variant of a permanent house guest at David and Melinda's apartment. He would often eat or do his laundry there and would watch their house when they were away, though no one was certain what was there to watch.

Before too long, Mark broke the lease on the apartment he shared near campus to move across town, quite a ways from MNC, but right down the block from Melinda. And, of course, his new friend David.

* * * *

David and Melinda fell into the typical routine of a young working couple without children. Neither was on any fast track at their jobs, but at least both their hours were regular. For the Harmons, work, though hardly salvation, was at least not an endless grind. They were truly blessed that Lambert had set them up in their adult lives.

David had his athletic endeavors after work and on weekends, and his regular Friday lunches with Kevin Jakabosky, the local paper salesman who moonlighted as a night-shift guard at a nearby lockup for juvenile delinquents. He also frequently lunched with his bank colleagues, at local sandwich and rib places and at their desks, where he would be good-naturedly reminded to watch what he ate. His suits began to pull and tug in all the wrong places, but David did not seem to care.

Over lunch he would regale the women at the bank with accounts of how Melinda would brighten at the gifts he gave her, even as the women wondered to themselves how he could continue to afford to keep this acquisitive woman happy. They had better manners than to say such a thing, of course. Besides, David was so endearingly earnest, so keen to notice her likes and dislikes, that if he spent a little too much on his wife, what was the harm in that?

Melinda was more of a letter writer than a gift giver. It was a dying art, but Melinda was single-handedly trying to revive it—even when she ought to have been finishing this task or that for the dean. There were a few complaints about her lack of professionalism at MNC, but none grievous enough to "eighty-six" the daughter of the general superintendent.

Melinda had little in the way of outside interests beyond work, life around the campus, and keeping house. She could have taken or audited classes, but did not. Together, the Harmons regularly attended to their church work, along with Bible study, on weekends. Melinda was dutiful, but when it came to taking food to families who had been down on their luck, church members knew David as the one with the activist spirit, the one who performed his charitable work with a bit more zest.

Although Melinda may not have had as much enthusiasm as David in helping the poor, she was more than willing to uphold other Nazarene standards.

In 1981, her boss, Dean Smith, was unexpectedly fired and replaced by Donald Stelting, an MNC history professor for four years and a former pastor. Though students were upset and puzzled over the decision to replace the popular dean, the founding president of the school, Dr. R. Curtis Smith (no relation) had to act quickly in response to a display of rank incompetence by Dean Smith. Word soon leaked that the president had received a tip that Jim Smith was having an affair with a secretary and that the dean had been fired for the offense—there was zero tolerance for such behavior at the Bible college. The campus newspaper, the *Trailblazer*, ran the scandal as its lead story and the affair was widely discussed, albeit in muted tones, around town.

The adulterous couple was turned in by an office secretary named Janelle Hansen and her co-worker and friend, Melinda Harmon.

* * * *

Gayle and Richard Bergstrand and their infant son lived side by side with the Harmons in a duplex along Route 7, a blacktop thoroughfare which, in the gathering state of Olathe's population, had been gaining traffic by the day.

Gayle was not unaware that Melinda, only a few years younger than herself, sometimes seemed a touch unhappy. Gayle wrote it off to the economic times, or perhaps trouble getting pregnant. Early on in a marriage—especially during this time of farms failing all around them and inflation on the march—there were always sacrifices to make, dreams to ratchet down. Gayle had never heard Melinda and David fighting, or seen them unhappy with one another. Marital troubles, on the whole, were not widely publicized within the church community. More realistically, Gayle assumed the Harmons were probably like a million other couples marrying early and settling down.

Gayle had noticed that their friend Mark came around with increasing frequency, but she did not give the friendship a second thought. Mark was, after all, also a good friend of David's. They were always on their way to and from sporting activities.

The Harmons ate frequently at the McDonald's near their apartment, which was not helping David's waistline. Melinda stayed thin and ever presentable. David seemed unconcerned about his appearance, and he'd use his emerging girth as fodder for self-deprecating jokes.

There began to be talk at the bank about how nobody saw Melinda that often. She wasn't impolite to them when they did see her; however, she was noticeably absent from a long string of bank events. Considering the close-knit nature of the Patron's Bank "family," as they called it, her absence was a curiosity.

David's friend Kevin, on his way to another night shift at the juvenile jail, would pass by the Harmon house along Route 7 and often furrow his brow when he saw Mark's car there so late. Was something amiss?

Melinda, meanwhile, busied herself writing letters of "friendship" to Mark, another curiosity, given the frequency with which he visited the Harmons' home.

1-31-81

I think more than anything what has hit me is that you will not be here after the first semester of next year.[1] Most likely, you will either be working or in graduate school somewhere out west. And that will pretty much drastically change things as they are now. Even though these changes are GOOD and they are normal, and they are part of the growing up process, they still do not come

---

1 The reference to Mark's leaving school early had to do with Mark toying with the idea of graduating early. Shortly thereafter, he reconsidered. Most of the letters were dropped in Mark's campus mail box unpostmarked. This letter was the only one dated, as Melinda had no reason to think she was writing for posterity.

easy for me. And really, this has bothered me somewhat. I want so much to be able to share these feelings with you. I am realizing that different students will come and go each year, and nothing will really stay the same for very long. This has just hit me kind of hard since the holidays . . .

Stability in the midst of things that are constantly changing (like emotions, situations, plans, feelings, circumstances, etc. . .) is something that is certainly worth striving for. There is nothing in life to compare this with.

This kind of sums up how I have been feeling. It doesn't really say much now, but emotions—it just helps me to write it down. Thanks you so much for being my "stable" friend.

Love You,
Melinda

Another note read:

Dear Mark:

Here I go again, trying to explain myself to you. Maybe I am too complex for my own good.

I find myself feeling very frustrated with our communication level at the moment, and rather than bottle it up, I'd like to get my feelings on paper. I received a letter from you last fall in which you told me how much our friendship meant to you. I keep telling myself that it's true, that you really feel this way now. Since that time, I have shared many things with you. Since the past few months have been extra difficult for me, I have unloaded on you many times with my feelings and concerns. As I look at it now, I have to wonder if it has been fair for me to do this to you. I have put your confidence and friendship above the student level . . .

Anyhow, I'm not even sure what I'm trying to say in this letter. Except that I just felt like writing some of my thoughts on paper. My thoughts and concerns go way beyond a "surface" level, Mark. My feelings go very deep, and I never want to be a shallow person. Sometimes I feel like you don't see this side of me, and I really want for you to . . .

I honestly believe that the Lord sends people our way for different times in our lives. I believe in all sincerity that you were a special gift from God (and still are). You were sent my way to make this year brighter for me. The Lord has really used you to minister to me!

Melinda

And this, written during revival week, which would keep Mark busy throughout, in late February 1982:

There are a lot of things I could say, and will in the future, but for today—the beginning of revival week—let me say I appreciate so much your testimony and spirituality. I hurt sometimes because I don't show my testimony very well to you. I worry about that! I want so much to be a help to you and never a spiritual hindrance. I hope you'll be enriched this week—I'll be praying and thinking about you.

Melinda.

* * * *

One February afternoon in 1982, Kevin picked David up for floor hockey. It was a day Mark wasn't playing. When they approached a red light, David uncharacteristically reached over and put a hand on Kevin's leg, then leaned his head back a moment and closed his eyes, as though he was about to confess something. Kevin was taken aback. David opened his eyes, saying nothing. After a pregnant pause, Kevin joked, "Dave, I'm not that kind of boy."

David laughed, and quickly removed his hand. Kevin waved the moment off and went about the rest of the day as though nothing had happened. Later, Kevin would replay this moment over and over in his mind, wishing to God he had only asked if anything was wrong.

A couple of weeks later, on Saturday, February 27, Mark and David started the day off with a fierce game of racquetball at a sports club the two had recently joined. The friends followed up their game with a stop at McDonald's. They picked up lunch, stopped at the bank so David could run in to get cash, and then returned to the Harmons' to eat.

When they arrived, Melinda was cleaning the house. She had also done Mark's laundry, which was something she often did for him when he lugged over a pile of dirty clothes. After lunch, David went off to do some work on one of his father-in-law's rental properties. Then he returned to the house to pick up Mark to play floor hockey. Mark begged off, though, claiming he had a stomachache from the McDonald's lunch. David went off to play, again leaving Mark alone with Melinda.

His teammates noticed that David seemed distracted. He played without his usual intensity. He let goals get past him like never before. Delvin Jakabosky, one of David's teammates, asked if Harmon could pass along a message to Mark. David, out of character, snapped back, "I'm not Mark's keeper."

That night, David and Melinda were expected for dinner at the home of Karen Hodges, their friend and fellow College Church of the Nazarene member. But the couple didn't show. It was unlike them, Karen thought at the time, because David and Melinda were generally a punctual and respectful young couple. Hodges tried to relegate her concern to idle worry, but she could not. David and Melinda showed too much deference to pull a no-show, especially on a fellow church member. Anything was possible, Hodges supposed, but there must have been a reason.

She called their apartment. There was no answer.

* * * *

Sometime in the middle of that night, Gayle Bergstrand heard heavy thudding noises coming from the Harmons' duplex next door. Sounds that were like a repeated smacking of meat. Twelve, maybe fourteen thuds? In two separate batches about a minute apart. She listened closer, going so far as to put her ear against the wall, but the commotion was followed by utter silence.

She woke Richard and explained what she had heard, but he told her not to worry. There must be an innocuous explanation for it all. It was surely just a stray sound from the street, or, at worst, David falling down the stairs.

Richard went back to sleep. Gayle did not. She focused on David tumbling down the stairs. David was big, she knew, but more than a dozen smacks and in two batches? Did he throw himself down the stairs once and, that being insufficient, climb back up to do it a second time for good measure?

Gayle roused Richard again. It could have been a noise from a train, or a car backfiring, he said. But she knew it wasn't a train or a car. Trying to figure out what she had heard on the other side of the wall filled Gayle with such foreboding that she was not by any leap of faith—or trust in Richard's intuition—going back to sleep.

She went into the other bedroom and lifted the baby from the crib. She noticed a light on in the backyard. And was that someone running outside?

Gayle went back to bed, now cradling her baby, next to her sleeping husband.

She was strangely relieved when, at about 3:30 A.M., someone rang her doorbell, followed by a series of desperate knocks on the door. At least one leg of the suspense was over. Though, to be sure, a whole new one would begin.

Gayle woke Richard with a well-directed kick. He went to the front door, opening it no more than a sliver.

Richard let Melinda in immediately.

David had been attacked, she said calmly, and she had been knocked out cold. By "blacks," she added, after giving them the keys to the front door of the bank where David worked.

Melinda's story didn't seem well-rehearsed, but it did sound too calm. In fact, considering how collected Melinda appeared, Gayle's first impression—despite having heard the sounds from the other side of the wall—was that Melinda was exaggerating. Was it humanly possible to be so restrained, Gayle asked herself, in the aftermath of an attack and burglary? Where was the panic? The slightest degree of breathlessness?

Melinda didn't say anything about David's condition, and Gayle didn't ask. Instead, Gayle called the police. She put her arm around Melinda, who was wearing a nightgown with a blanket wrapped around her shoulders. Gayle asked what else she could do. Melinda told her to call an aunt and uncle who, along with so many of her relatives, had recently migrated to Olathe. Gayle dialed the number but the uncle and aunt either weren't home or were able to sleep through the endless rings.

"Oh," Melinda said casually. "Try Mark." She knew his number by heart.

Melinda told Gayle the same story she would soon tell police. She awoke in bed to the sound of David being beaten by two black men. She was then pulled downstairs to the living room. One man said to the other, "I think you hit him too hard. You may have killed him."

They forced Melinda to hand over the bank keys, which were sitting in a dish, then struck her, knocking her out.

Mark arrived ten minutes after Gayle called, appearing freshly showered and wearing a corduroy blazer. By now a large group of police officers, including a crime-scene photographer and several detectives, had arrived. Paul Morrison, an ambitious assistant district attorney, was among the first on the scene. He was led up the staircase to the bedroom. Paul could see a blood spatter that ran halfway down the hallway outside of the bedroom. In the room, on the bed, face up, with the blankets pulled up around him, was David.

At first glance, Paul couldn't tell for sure whether the person lying dead on that bed was a man or a woman. He stood there fixated, watching a plume of foamy blood still swirling in David's mouth. As if he were still alive.

It was Paul's first murder scene. He needed air.

Outside on the patio, sucking in the cool Kansas wind, Paul turned toward the patio door. There was no sign of forced entry. Leaving that door unlocked at night along the busy Route 7 would take a foolish amount of trust in the goodness of passing strangers, even in such a small town. Mark's fingerprints would be found on the patio door, though there was no way to tell whether they were left there on the night of the murder.

Paul went next door. There he found Mark comforting his friend. For a woman who claimed to have been knocked unconscious for over an hour, Melinda was up and about with apparent ease, a fact that didn't escape Paul's attention or that of the other investigators at the scene. The bruise on her cheek (could someone be knocked out by a bruise to the cheek?) was slight. Paul had to squint to see the mark. His suspicions were roused.

Back at the Harmons' apartment, James Bridges, the coroner, removed David's bloody pajama top with his bare hands. He always worked crime scenes barehanded. And he worked—in his official capacity—out of the back of Frye's Funeral Home, often eating donuts during examinations of the dead.

"You're not worried about him thrashing around?" someone called out, with dark crime-scene humor.

"I think he was asleep," Bridges responded, in no mood to joke. Rick Lees, another Olathe cop, snapped pictures.

David's body was on the left side of the bed. The killer had landed the brunt of the blows around David's eyes and nose, which were caved in. The way blood was spattered to the left, even all the way outside of the bedroom and down the hall, seemed to indicate that the murderer, with long and powerful arms, had stood on the right side of the bed, possibly reaching over Melinda as he bludgeoned her husband, though the blood soaking her pillow made it unlikely that she had occupied her side of the bed. Maybe he was looking to gain distance to avoid getting bloodied. Or maybe he needed a few feet to remove himself, in spirit, from the deed. David's body had no defensive wounds, a fact that formed the basis for Bridges' conclusion that David had been asleep, presumably on his back, when he was attacked.

This meant the killer had a free and open look at the victim's face before striking the first blow. Judging by the condition of David's barely recognizable face, this was a crime of passion. Were it not for the pillow behind it, David's head might conceivably have been knocked off his neck.

The murder weapon must have been an instrument of blunt force. Something heavy and swingable, capable of inflicting brutal damage with crisp efficiency. A crowbar seemed likely. Or perhaps a 12-gauge shotgun fired at close range. The first police officers to arrive at the scene, reacting to the fact that David's face was completely pulverized, had reported when calling for additional personnel that the victim had been shot.

Either that, someone at the scene joked, or he was run over by a truck.

Gary Dirks was a forensic scientist at the Johnson County Crime Lab, but it did not take formal training to see that the placement of the body seemed a touch staged. Before the coroner removed David's pajama top, revealing the victim's midsection, Dirks noted that the bed sheets had been pulled up around Harmon's shoulders. There was blood under the sheets, indicating that the sheets had been moved after the blows were struck and blood sprayed.

Dirks also couldn't find so much as a single strand of "negroid hair," as he called it, anywhere in the Harmons' duplex. There seemed to be blood on the lower portion of the shower curtain. Had the killers stopped to soap up before they left the house?

Joseph C. Pruett, a warhorse of an Olathe detective and a real cowboy, quite literally, was conducting interviews at the Bergstrands' house. The old generation of detectives like Pruett (who himself favored Stetsons) wore cowboy hats, cowboy boots, the whole bit. Mark emphasized to Pruett that his arrival so soon after David's murder suggested no darker motive than to help one friend and mourn another. After all, the Harmons had taken him under their wing.

The way Paul saw it, Mark, composed and smartly dressed, was way too confident. Paul wondered where that crowbar was hidden, but there had clearly been time to get rid of it.

During their initial questioning, Mark and Melinda both told Pruett that while they were alone in the Harmon house, while David was off playing floor hockey with the Jakabosky brothers, they had taken separate naps.

Separate naps?

An attractive young man, the runaway hit of his college campus, and an equally attractive young woman, alone, while her chubby husband was off playing a boy's game. Pruett wasn't born yesterday.

Pruett noted the presence of a strange document that had been found in the Harmons' bedroom, on Melinda's nightstand. Melinda had apparently taken a letter from the disciplinary file of a student at the Bible college and brought it home. In the letter a student had threatened to smash someone's skull in:

> *When you came and butted in on my phone call today, and then got smart and unplugged the phone, my old nature wanted to smash your head in. But . . . the feeling didn't come across me too strongly. At the time, as I think about it, the more I can see how the situation could have developed into a bloody mess. Very bloody.*
>
> *And I believe it was the grace of God—a miracle—that didn't allow that to happen. This incident showed for sure my heart feelings for you today, that I do love you and don't need to fight with you. But I pray that if you ever provoke me again that way, God's grace and miraculous intervention will again save*

me from sin. . . . .God only knows what would happen if I just let you provoke me to uncontrolled madness. If you don't want something like that to happen, then I hope you will suppress any more actions like you did today. I sure don't need the temptation of taking a bat to your head, and I should think you wouldn't either.

Not your typical bedside reading material. Pruett considered that it could be a coincidence that this letter was lying around the house. But Bible school could be a deceptively charged place, and Pruett made a note to check the alibi of the student in question.

And separate naps?

*   *   *   *

Patrolman J. A. Larrick drove Gayle Bergstrand and Mark and Melinda, not yet official suspects, from the crime scene to the Olathe police station in a police cruiser.

Other than Melinda, Gayle was the closest the investigators had to a witness. She thought back to a day that summer when Richard had said he thought he had seen Mark and Melinda kissing or embracing at the neighborhood pool.

Now all she saw was tension.

"I am just so sorry," Melinda said to Mark in the back seat.

"You have nothing to apologize to me for," Mark snapped.

It was an ill-placed flash of temper. The rest of the five-minute ride was full of dumbfounded silence. Gayle thought of her baby and husband, who were still at home, just a few thin layers of sheetrock away from the crime scene.

But what had, in fact, happened? Gayle wanted more than anything to know how David was and was puzzled to realize that she didn't have an inkling. Despite all the EMTs at the Harmon duplex and in their own, Melinda had never once asked after David's condition or fate or whatever was the appropriate terminology for such a surreal turn.

At the station house, Gayle watched as Reverend Cunningham approached Melinda. Gayle approached a patrolman. "How is David?" she asked.

"Oh, he's dead," the patrolman answered.

It looked to Gayle as if Rev. Cunningham was delivering the same news to Melinda, though while Gayle stood crying, Melinda, like some figure in a nightmare, remained composed.

Soon, Larrick conducted the first interview—with Gayle, Melinda, and Mark together at the same time, a glaring breach of protocol. Pruett got to the station at about 5 A.M. Larrick briefed him, then Pruett separated the three and interviewed Melinda alone. She repeated her original story. He asked to keep the nightgown as evidence. After he finished the interview, Pruett checked with a supervisor, Lieutenant Jeff Herrmann, who told him to release Melinda. She was picked up by cousins and brought to their home.

Meanwhile, Mark's story was hardly airtight. He had been home alone, he said, just blocks from the murder scene. He arrived at the scene soon after the killing, but only because he had been summoned. And, no, he told investigators repeatedly, he was not freshly showered, though he could not dispute the fact that he arrived in the middle of the night dressed in a corduroy sports coat, which seemed an odd choice of clothing to grab as one is running out of one's home in the middle of the night on a moment's notice upon hearing that one's good friend was murdered. Also, Mark insisted, the fact that some thought Melinda was less distraught than they might have expected—or preferred—should have no bearing on him. But it did. As did his own oddly calm comportment.

Mark granted permission for police to search his apartment that morning. With his permission came two admissions. In a metal box they would find about two dozen letters from Melinda. They were not love letters, just notes from one friend to another. The police were welcome to examine them. Mark also informed the police that he had soiled his pants that night. What had happened that night, Pruett wondered, to cause a grown man, a big man on campus, to shit himself? A bad case of indigestion, which he blamed on the McDonald's meal, Mark told a now openly skeptical Pruett.

In his first interview, Mark made one of his few lapses. He failed to mention that he and Melinda, while taking a walk on the day of the murder, stopped back at his apartment. Melinda had mentioned it in her interview, however. When Pruett asked about this walk in Mark's next interview, Mark said it was for an emergency trip to the bathroom. Was this additional evidence of an affair, or the same innocent bout of diarrhea that caused him to soil his pants?

The following day, Mark's brother Ray found Mark a pseudo-lawyer, Fred Jones,[2] a friend of Ray's who hoped to go to law school. The only advice he gave Mark was to continue cooperating with the police.

---

2 Because of his standing as an active FBI agent, this name is a pseudonym.

Back at the duplex, the investigation continued, lead by Detective Roger LaRue. There wasn't an armload of evidence to remove from David and Melinda's apartment, and despite the expanding perimeter that investigators searched, which included sewers and woods, no murder weapon was found in the pre-dawn dark. Hours later, the morning of February 28, a dog followed a scent from the Harmons' patio door to a dumpster behind Mark's apartment. No evidence was found. A search party was then dispatched to the town dump to conduct the unpleasant task of canvassing mountains of trash.

Later that afternoon, LaRue and his partner Howard Kannady went to 1404 Salem Street to visit the home of Hardy Weathers—a Lambert cousin who was a minister at the College Church and would, in good time, rise to become "head of publishing" for the national Nazarene Church—to re-interview Melinda. The Lamberts, who now lived in Ohio, were staying as guests there.

LaRue had been raised a Christian, but not an evangelical one. Recently, after his divorce, he had joined the Nazarenes to take advantage of their counseling services for his two young boys. He knew this Harmon boy from church; though, as infrequently as it happened, it was not atypical in Olathe to know the victim of a crime personally. David and Melinda seemed like a nice, young, observant couple, though she did have slight airs. She did not exercise restraint in letting you know who her father was. She was also known to be conspicuously uninhibited, overly affectionate and flirtatious, though besides that, LaRue had not heard a bad word about her that he could remember. Pride in your father was surely a forgivable sin.

Less forgivable to LaRue was the fact that no one had leaned hard enough on Melinda the night of the murder. She had been interviewed three times—once at the Bergstrand home and then twice at the station—and Melinda's story was the same each time. Melinda had been treated as a grieving widow and the police, doubly cautious because of her father's stature in the community, had failed to challenge her. In fact, the bank was already being staked out for the two black suspects. LaRue realized Melinda's story was full of holes, and he intended to press her to explain them. The Church discouraged divorce, along with birth control, and Melinda knew better than anyone the result of a scandalous affair. Was it possible that she actually believed murder to be preferable? Less sinful?

At the house, the detectives were met at the door not by Weathers, but by "the huge wheel" himself, Melinda's father.

"Good afternoon, Mr. Lambert," said LaRue.

"It's *Dr.* Lambert," was the reply. "She is not talking to any of you without my being there," Lambert said, standing a bit too close to LaRue for his comfort.

LaRue knew he had to tread carefully here, and Lambert was adamant—to the point of abrasiveness.

"She has not been treated with the proper respect," Lambert said to Roger, who already felt she had been treated with too much. The likeable, neighborly Weathers was also acting as bouncer. This was turning into an interrogation on the installment plan.

Against their better judgment, the detectives agreed to let Lambert attend the interview. They went upstairs to a bedroom where Melinda was lying down, propped on pillows, covered by a blanket. The three men surrounded the bed.

"You don't have to answer anything you don't want to," Lambert barked at Melinda.

She gave a trace of a nod and LaRue reviewed what had happened. She was slow to answer his questions initially, wearing almost a sedated expression. He asked her to repeat what happened. She said she had been awakened by ungodly sounds and, hardly able to draw a breath, had been dragged downstairs where she was eventually knocked unconscious, but not before hearing the two men discussing how they thought they had killed her husband. They took the bank keys, too, before knocking her to the ground. LaRue looked at the small bruise on her cheek.

When the detectives questioned a detail in her story—whether that patio door had been locked or not—she twitched both feet under the covers.

Lambert, either a comfort or a saboteur, tossed a throw pillow on her. Bewildered, close to tears, Melinda said she couldn't be of any more help. "I blacked out and then I woke up, and I don't know if the doors were locked or not when I went to the Bergstrands."

And the letters? Chaste expressions of friendship. Nazarenes always signed their notes "Love." As in, Love thy neighbor.

Conveniently, Lambert answered several of the follow-up questions for Melinda, and the detectives left with the same story she had given the night before.

Back outside the bedroom, Roger asked Lambert who may have wanted to kill his son-in-law.

"I don't know," he said. "I have no idea."

"Were David and Melinda having troubles?" LaRue asked.

"Most definitely not. Their marriage appeared good," Lambert replied. "Of course," he continued as LaRue leaned in, "David was not the sort to tell Melinda if he was having trouble with anyone." Lambert paused again. "And in one of my rental properties—one he helps care for—we had a black tenant who left without paying rent. That was before David starting caring for the place, but . . ."

Another black suspect? Or perhaps the same one, one of the pair that might be, this very moment, converging on the bank only to be greeted by a heavily armed welcoming committee.

In the presence of Lambert, LaRue didn't ask the questions burning in his mind: Why did the beatings occur in two batches? How could she be sleeping beside David when the blows started but only have blood spatter on the lower portion of her nightgown? Why would thieves steal keys to a bank when everyone knows front door keys can't get you into a vault? Why would these two thieves beat one victim with such fury and give the other one little more than a love tap? If there was blood in the shower, had the murderers taken time to clean up at the scene? Had Melinda really been knocked out for about an hour by a strike to the cheek before running to neighbors, while maintaining good recall of the trauma that had just befallen her? How about the letter that carried with it a promise to bash a head in? Standard bedside reading?

The questions would have to wait for another time, LaRue decided.

Other leads were quickly tumbling in. Police headquarters' open phone lines, an instrumental part of any investigation, were ringing. The murder had spread a current of fear—even temporary madness— around Olathe. People were boarding up windows and arming themselves. In the initial hours and days after the murder, the public desperately wanted it solved.

There was a "fag" who worked at the bank. David, who had teased him about his sexual orientation, had pointed to him for a theft of about $1,000 in cash. In turn, the man had insulted David about his weight. That this bank employee could go from jests about fat hips to wanton murder seemed a stretch, though the disappearing money was an intriguing angle of investigation, as was "the lunatic" investigators soon heard about—a man who had worked on computers at Patron's for a while, gone to MNC for a time, and bizarrely, began shouting out well-known details about the murder to anyone who'd listen. He'd later be committed to an insane asylum, but at the time he seemed to be another relevant avenue of investigation.

A couple of phantom black men, a co-worker with a grudge, a raving lunatic, and an imbalanced letter-writing student. These were the "leads" LaRue had to go on. The best option still seemed to be a fourth interview with Melinda.

The search at the dump for the murder weapon went on for days. But even carting in klieg lights to illuminate every piece of trash didn't help. By March 3, police aborted the search.

Searches of David and Melinda's cars—a Chevy Caprice Classic and a Chevy Monza—came back empty. Investigators searched Mark's car too, a true period piece in the form of a 1970 black Pontiac LeMans four-door with green vinyl. In the trunk was a sweatshirt covered in streaks of mud that seemed to match the mud on the pair of jeans police had found in his apartment. Mark said he had repaired a spigot that day with David, but this, along with the soiled jockeys, raised eyebrows. One of the Jakabosky brothers called after he was interviewed by the police to say he thought he remembered seeing a crowbar in Mark's trunk recently, but vague, wooly memories about possible murder weapons did as much good for the investigation as the whole lot of nothing found at the dump.

A report of screeching tires the night of the murder around the Harmon duplex was investigated, but could not be linked to Mark's LeMans. A midnight security guard who, along with his brother, was headed over to his sister's place on Edgemere, near the Harmons, to quell a domestic disturbance, saw a red vehicle speed by at forty miles per hour. The brothers remembered it well, because they cursed the car heartily. The timing did not fit that of the murder, and the car color did not match up with Mark's.

Someone developed a theory that David might have been beaten with the removable midsection of the Harmons' washing machine, which could then have been reinserted and the machine run to remove the blood. But no evidence was found to support this idea.

One of the more intriguing theories developing in the investigation was that homosexuality was involved. David and Mark had spent a lot of time together. And Mark had not, to anyone's knowledge, ever slept with a woman. Further weight was given to this theory when police interviewed

Amy Morton, an intoxicatingly pretty second-semester sophomore, the day after the murder. The Salina, Kansas, girl, who ran cross-county track at the school, dated Mark for a year until he broke it off, right around Christmas. Their typical date came once a week, when they'd go together to take in some Christian singing. When asked if her former boyfriend was effeminate, Amy nodded "yes" without hesitation.

"When I first met him, I thought he was gay," she said. She was a virgin, she added, and Mark never made anything in the way of a sexual advance. Their last date had been two weeks before the murder, off campus at the Smokestack restaurant. Then they went to his LeMans where he said they should see other people. Amy was confused—confused about the lack of advances (not that she would have consented to anything), and confused at the sudden break up.

Contradicting the gay hypothesis, there was no way to dial down the suspicions of an affair between Mark and Melinda. Janelle Hansen, who had, along with Melinda, turned in Dean Smith for his adulterous affair, had warned Melinda that a "dangerous situation" was developing between her and Mark. Melinda laughed it off as a harmless flirtation, but Janelle couldn't hide her scorn at the way Melinda kept one phone line in her office open just for Mark's calls.

There was also the fact that Melinda would receive $40,000 in life insurance. The Harmons, as Gayle Bergstrand had noticed, had not been having an easy time financially. Sure enough, between late October in 1981 and that last week of February in 1982, David and Melinda's main checking account had been overdrawn five times. A second checking account had all of ten dollars in it.

Police had, in a matter of days, cleared the "fag" and the "lunatic" who had worked at the bank, along with the author of the note that Melinda kept bedside, of any wrongdoing. They all had solid alibis. Even Ray Mangelsdorf, who police heard was the brother capable of the deed, was investigated, but his alibi of smoking pot with friends checked out. The Barnes brothers, a pair of black ex-cons working the Kansas City area, were interviewed, but that lead likewise went nowhere. And the two key thieves never did show up for the payday they had supposedly killed for.

With little else panning out and suspicion still heavily centered on Mark and Melinda, LaRue went to talk to Melinda yet again, this time with a new partner named Dwight Cobb. She was now officially considered a suspect. Along with the crime-scene chat and the questions at the police station afterward, this would be their second pass at a home-visit interview with her. LaRue was troubled not only by the accumulation of evidence, as soft and slight as it was, but also by his instinct. The whole time at the Bergstrand house on the night of the murder, Melinda had never once asked after her husband's condition, an indication that she already knew he was dead. And while her ill-fated husband was off working at her father's properties, was this desirable young woman really doing housework while that big man on campus nursed a bellyache, before they went off to take separate naps?

This time, it was over to Cambridge Street, where the Lamberts were staying at the home of V. H. Lewis, the noted Nazarene pastor and David's favorite author. David had spent hours upon hours in his home, as he and Lewis talked about faith and the good works they planned to do.

Lewis was on a mission in Africa at the time of the murder. LaRue and Cobb opened the house's screen door and rang the doorbell. Another Lambert cousin opened the inner door; this one visiting from Oakland, California. "Oh no, boys, not now, this is not the time," he said, then slammed the door directly on their faces and locked it.

"There are places," LaRue said to Cobb, "where if you slam a door in an officer's face, you lose that door."

Shortly after that, Dr. Lambert came to the door, unlocked it, and admitted the officers. The family was apparently having a private meeting. Dr. Lambert escorted the detectives to the library, where LaRue told him that new information had developed and they would need to talk to Melinda again.

After a brief and heated discussion, Melinda was brought to the library and asked to come to the sheriff's office.

"I'll go," she said. Lambert announced he would come as well, along with the visiting cousin. When the group got to police headquarters, stashed in a building with other city offices, they took the elevator to the fifth floor. When they stepped off the elevator, LaRue attempted to separate Melinda from her father.

LaRue told Lambert, "Melinda's going to have to be questioned closely. And read her rights."

"The hell she will," said Lambert. "She's coming home with me and right now you bumbling pieces of shit," he said, advancing at LaRue, pushing a forefinger into his chest, again and again and again.

In any other circumstance, LaRue, a Vietnam veteran who had killed in combat and had no squeamishness about doling out punishment, would have reacted with equal aggression and might have charged Lambert with interfering with an investigation or even with assaulting a police officer.

Instead, an assistant district attorney, Mike Buser, rushed out of his office to assuage Lambert, still seething and shouting about the "stupid shit" detectives. A compromise was promptly offered. Melinda would be interviewed but, again, only in Lambert's presence.

In the interview room, LaRue told Melinda—who observed the events around her passively, like a bystander at an accident—that she was a suspect. She was read her rights. She said she understood and wanted to talk.

LaRue gave Lambert a form to sign as a witness. He threw the paper back at LaRue, unsigned.

"Is she actually being considered a suspect?" Lambert asked.

"She is, in the way everyone is," LaRue said.

Lambert had heard enough. He literally grabbed Melinda by the shirt, sneered again that the detectives were "stupid shits," and walked his daughter to the elevator. Jeff Herrmann, LaRue's supervisor, called after Lambert that they would need to discuss this matter at length, but nobody stopped Lambert and Melinda as they walked out the front door.

What should have been the definitive interview—Melinda had even been read her rights—had degenerated into farce. Melinda had not been asked a single question. Through simple bluster and the inimitable power of his standing in the community, Lambert had chaperoned his daughter right out of LaRue's clutches. LaRue and other detectives discussed charging Lambert, but such talk went nowhere.

Despite repeated attempts, LaRue had been unable to get more than a few words with a chief suspect, and this raised disturbing suspicions about exactly why the volatile Lambert was allowed to exert such influence.

To LaRue, though, the message from above, from the district attorney's office, was clear—make every attempt not to be capricious with Lambert, considering who he was. Do not antagonize him. Do not risk an adversarial exchange. Since such exchanges are normally part and parcel of good police work, were the authorities giving the murderer or murderers a pass?

* * * *

James Bridges, the old-line country police coroner famous for working corpses without gloves out of the back of Frye Funeral Home (often while perching a cigar on the examination slab) termed the once fit and muscular David "obese" on the autopsy report. David weighed in at 260 pounds. The fact that the once aspiring athlete, so handsome and fit, was labeled obese at the end of his short life was nearly as disturbing, to those who knew David and read the report, as the description of his injuries. The wounds, the report said, had been inflicted with extreme vehemence, and as a result had a peculiar contoured quality, which meant that many of the blows had dug in extra deep. The killer or killers must have used some sort of club with an extension, or a crowbar.

John and Sue, David's parents, were at home in Chili on Sunday, February 28, when they received the call from Hardy Weathers, the

Lambert cousin. Initially, for an altogether random reason, John assumed that David had fallen off a ladder. Had he told him not to climb a ladder? He could not have fathomed the truth.

But there was no ladder, and no accident. Hardy Weathers was soon telling him that David was dead, murdered in his sleep, and there would be a funeral in two days. The drive from Chili to Olathe is over a thousand miles, and John and Sue would never be there in time for the funeral, which Melinda, they learned, had refused to delay. She couldn't even wait for David's mentor, Lewis, who was returning from his missionary trip on Wednesday, only one day after the funeral. David was to be buried fast, though this wasn't a Nazarene tradition.

The Harmons would have needed to wait until Monday for the banks to open to get cash for the trip, were it not for the donation of money by their church that enabled them to catch a plane immediately.

David's funeral was a short and strange affair at College Church in Olathe. The ceremony attracted a nearly unprecedented five hundred people. At the funeral, John and Sue were shuttled away from the front row and were not allowed near Melinda. Melinda, under the watchful eyes of the police, was sobbing convulsively as she came down the aisle. In the front pew, she leaned her head on Mark's shoulder. He whispered something into her ear. What had he said?

At the funeral, Melinda seemed close to a broken woman, ready to fold. It stood to reason, even to the untrained observer, that if the police had simply been willing or competent enough to get her alone, to interview her not in several short bursts but in one long, grueling drag, she would have, in some attempt at repentance, told all. But

Melinda left Olathe immediately after the hasty fifteen-minute burial at nearby Oak Lawn cemetery, never to return.

That same day, Mark dropped his pseudo lawyer. School and church officials got him a new lawyer: Hugh Kreamer. Mark stopped talking to the authorities altogether. Kreamer was a bigwig attorney who was dying of cancer but had recently served for three terms as Johnson Country District Attorney. Mark's case would be his very last. He was helped along by his son, Scott, a sharp risk taker who had once raced Formula Atlantic cars in Canada but had come home to Olathe to practice law.

The involvement of the high-profile Kreamers, legal royalty in Johnson County, only increased tension in the police department. In the early days of the investigation it seemed inevitable that someone would be arrested immediately. But no arrests had been made, and the public was furious.

Pressure from the media and the frightened citizens of Olathe began to mount. To move justice along, in early March, the Metro Squad from the Kansas Bureau of Investigation, the state's top investigation squad, was brought in to assist in the case. They were heralded by headlines in the *Olathe News*. Finally, the reporters wrote with sure-fire conviction, the KBI—unlike the local yokels—would get to the bottom of the case. Those wakeful, fear-filled nights in Olathe were soon to be over.

Mark was now being watched by both the Olathe police and the Metro Squad, who were trying to unsettle him by stopping him for imagined traffic infractions, sometimes roughly, even to the point of throwing him up against his car. Mark was harassed daily.

The KBI questioned all the people who fell into David and Melinda's social circle, which amounted to quite a few students.

Chris Launius, a friend of Mark's from high school and, as vice president of the student body at the Bible college, the second in command on campus, had spent time at the Harmon home, though not, admittedly, on the day of the murder. The police gave him the treatment.

But Chris had the ultimate alibi. As part of his senior term project, Chris had spent the night of the murder in a nunnery.

LaRue was surprised to find the students at the college so reluctant to discuss the case, until he learned from Gayle Bergstrand's husband, Richard, precisely why the students were so tight-lipped. Richard was taking classes at the college at the time of the murder. Though a Methodist, he was a pharmacist looking to go to medical school and trying to pick up some needed biology credits. An announcement came in biology class that students were not to talk to anyone about the murder case under any circumstances. The message, even if not overtly stated, was that Nazarenes, as a group, were under attack. The best response to protecting their insular way of life was silence.

LaRue was also being greeted with disdain at church—the church he had shared with David, and still shared with Mark and Melinda. LaRue found many acrimonious detractors in the pews. The dirty looks during Sunday services became familiar. One woman, calling LaRue a blessed shame, said he should be spending his time corralling the black killers, not harassing his fellow Nazarenes. The tension, the current of madness that ran through the church, was a lot for a good Christian to overcome.

Public opinion in Olathe was split down the middle. While most Nazarenes simply couldn't imagine that an upstanding young man like Mark could commit such an inexplicably heinous crime, the old-time Olathe residents thought Mark was guilty and accused the Nazarenes of standing close-mouthed through it all. Not only did this increasingly powerful Nazarene constituency seem to be obstructing the investigation, they were showing signs of actually leaning on Dennis Moore, the district attorney, not to act. Moore, who had his sights set on Congress, didn't seem to have any qualms about accommodating the Nazarenes. Some of the farmers, whose ancestral plains were destined to be carved up into subdivisions before long, suspected the newcomers of fencing out the truth for fear of disgracing the Bible college around which they were building their community.

To the old timers, and even some Nazarenes, the incriminating details began to mount. There were the letters, the soiled underwear, a report of a vacuum cleaner running in the middle of the night in Mark's apartment, Mark's lack of a solid alibi, and what appeared to be a circling of wagons by the college community.

Additionally, LaRue had moles in the Nazarene church. One was Reverend Paul G. Cunningham, the head pastor and police department cleric held in suspicion by many outside the church. Cunningham was ever present during the investigation and also offered comfort to Melinda alongside the likes of Lambert and Weathers. He did not speak publicly in support of the investigation, which made his support only marginally useful, yet he was not exclusively on Lambert's side either. It was he who suggested LaRue interview Jim Smith, the former college dean Melinda had turned in for having an affair.

When LaRue arrived at Smith's new post, a high school south of Olathe, Smith told the detective, "I'm surprised you weren't here sooner. I was expecting you."

Smith gave Mark ringing endorsements, but felt Melinda was nervous and unstable. Though older than Mark, Melinda was less self-possessed, less sincere. "I'm not trying to drive a wooden stake through her heart," Smith said, "but she is different."

But even with his misgivings and suspicions, he had nothing substantive to give LaRue. Thanks to Melinda, he had not been on campus for quite a while.

The Harmons, for their part, went back to Chili. They could not linger in Olathe forever, as John had his students to get back to. The Harmons would only hear from Melinda once more, nine months after their son's murder, in a note sent from her parents' home in Ohio before Christmas:

> Dear Mom & Dad H:
> It was great to hear from you, I appreciate that. I have not been doing well at all, and so I haven't been writing to ANYBODY. It is just too much emotionally for me I guess. But I really wanted to send you this note to tell you how very much I do love you, need you, pray for you, think of you. There are no words that can convey the grief we are sharing. I know, but I feel that we can love & pray for one another. I would love to hear from you. Please be assured of my love & prayers for you.
> Melinda

* * * *

The Metro Squad left after less than a week, and the Olathe detectives were put back in charge. Some felt that Metro had been parachuted in for a mere political show, without ever intending to stay long enough or work hard enough to solve the crime. Whatever the case, Olathe police resumed their investigation by consulting Carol Dawn, a psychic who lived over the Missouri line in Independence. In the hope that the psychic could divine something useful, Joy Hempy, David's dear friend at the bank, had provided a pink felt-tipped pen that David had once used. The psychic was not able to help.

At the end of March, John Harmon called from Chili with new information. In the toolbox he had retrieved from David's duplex, he found a pry bar with an edge that could possibly have been used in the murder. The bar was sent over to the Monroe County Crime Lab, and the matter was never heard of again.

LaRue and the other officers kept hassling Mark, but he never broke. Because Mark felt so hounded, he moved from his apartment to take refuge in the home of Dean Stelting, the man who had replaced Jim Smith. Stelting's house became the site of a constant stake-out, thrilling the dean's young boys, Don and Damon.

Mark tried to fight back against the rumors by demonstrating his efforts to continue living his life as best he could. One afternoon, on the knoll that stood just out of range of the long shadow of the College Church steeple, Mark breathlessly approached Kevin Jakabosky.

"You have to understand," said Mark, his chest heaving, having run across the campus from church to tell Kevin, who had not asked and was trying his best not to hear what had taken place that night. Or, more to the point, what had *not* taken place.

Mark caught his breath. "I know what is being said, but I had nothing to do with what happened to David," Mark said. "He was my friend. You know, I hate that people treat me bad. I don't—there's a lot of things going on here—a lot of explanations. I don't want my brothers mad at me."

Then Mark asked if he could come to floor hockey that day, only the third session held since David last played. The request made Kevin uneasy. His brother Delvin was convinced Mark was guilty, and the team was playing at the Christian high school where Delvin was a teacher. Kevin, looking to accommodate Mark, invited him anyway. When Mark got there, he saw David's lefty pad and glove hanging, in tribute, on the support bars of a basketball hoop. Mark was ignored by David's teammates and left before the game began.

Mark continued to live with the Steltings for the rest of the semester, completing his studies and fulfilling both his academic and student body presidential responsibilities with, as a caption from their senior yearbook noted, "warmth and guidance" and an ability to "keep his cool as pressures from the job mount up."

A final order of business came on the very last day of school. Mark worked up the courage to ask out Susi Johnson, who would have been justified in being a bit skeptical about keeping company with Mark. Soon the two were dating. Her decision to go steady with Mark both did and did not surprise those who knew Susi. It was probably the one act in her life that was born of emotional spontaneity. Susi, who grew up outside of Olathe and used words like "pooey" on the rare occasion when she grew upset, was known as an endearing naïf.

She was dark haired and pretty in an unadorned way and, like Mark, was a prominent student at MNC. Her earnest work in the classroom, enthusiastic membership in a traveling Christian singing group, and constant effort toward the greater good made her a natural recipient of the Pioneer Award, given annually to one male and one female senior who best represented the ideals of higher learning and Christ on campus. And who was the male winner of the Pioneer Award?

Mark Mangelsdorf.

A picture in their senior yearbook shows Mark and Susi by a tree, just before their romance began. Mark, hands folded, dressed in a sport jacket and striped tie, is smiling for the camera, with a satisfied expression that looked out at the future with good humor, even a bit of humility, and all the attendant excitement of that moment in life when you are poised to enter the real world. And there is Susi, clear-eyed in a heavy, long dress, a woman steeped in the past and perhaps more complacent than contemplative, looking beside her at the boy who would soon become her husband.

* * * *

In May of 1983, a month before Mark and Susi married, the plains flooded—biblically, some said. The waters poured into the basement of Olathe City Hall, where, as fate would have it, the police evidence room sat. Evidence—and no one knows what or how much of it—was destroyed. The David Harmon files, marked damaged, had to be set out to dry and then resealed in a new cardboard box. There they sat, for almost two decades, almost forgotten. A case that had torn this small corner of Kansas asunder faded into memory.

PART TWO

"The wealth of the rich is their fortified city; they imagine it an unscalable wall."

—Proverbs 18:11

Four

Mark Mangelsdorf developed, over time, a singular place in the annals of Olathe history. He stayed on—to his credit, some felt—and despite being interrogated at length, trailed around Olathe, and thrown atop cars by police officers at traffic stops, he graduated with distinction from MNC. Mark could take comfort in the fact that the investigation had slowed to a crawl, and he was enjoying the unwavering support of his fellow Nazarenes. When Dean Donald E. Stelting bestowed the Pioneer Award upon Mark with a firm handshake, the class gave Mark a standing ovation.

Some people felt differently, of course. One vocal dissenter was local newspaper writer Andy Hoffman, who had a shock of white hair and a long finger pointed at a Nazarene attempt to cover up the involvement of one of their own. And then there were the members of Olathe's old guard, including the circle of women who had worked with David at Patron's Bank, who scoffed at how the Nazarenes had stood and cheered for a suspected murderer. The police had their suspicions but, with no bankable leads or significant evidence to implicate Mark beyond a reasonable doubt, they were helpless.

Like most recent college graduates, Mark was a few thin dimes away from flat broke. His future, though, was on a quick upward trajectory. Obscure Kansas Bible colleges are not a traditional stepping stone to Harvard Business School, but the big Ivy League college accepted Mark. He deferred for a year and crossed the state line into Missouri, where he landed an internship at a shipping concern. Mark excelled at the job. With an acceptance letter to Harvard in his back pocket (he chose Harvard over Stanford), Mark was keenly aware that while he was already a well-rounded student with many skills, and possessed the ability to learn faster than most, the real key to his success lay in mastering that most American of secular disciplines: business.

Almost a year after graduation, Mark and Susi were married before heading east to Cambridge, Massachusetts.

Soon Mark was listening with rapt attention to such entrepreneurial luminaries as Mary Kay Ash, the cosmetics magnate and sales innovator known for her fleet of pink Cadillacs, as a guest lecturer in his Power and Influence class. Adjusting to the mores of the East Coast Establishment was not easy for Mark, who was accustomed to getting by on instinct and intuition and who had, by and large, lived a cloistered existence. His fellow MBA candidates at Harvard were born into privilege, and most of them viewed Kansas, Missouri, and the surrounding swaths of the Midwest as a mysterious badlands.

Mark was initially seen as a Bible Belt curiosity, a big, earnest man loping around campus, who during his early days at business school did a bit of religious evangelizing, preaching the good word of Jesus Christ right in Harvard Yard. There were no smears, just an initial round of avoidance and trepidation at the unfamiliar. Classmates were soon impressed, though, by the way Mark absorbed the latest word on the vanguard of managerial thought, and by the mannerly Kansan's obvious instinct to avail himself of opportunities. Though he did not become a Baker Scholar, a designation given to a student in the highest five percent of the class, Mark was among the top students, notable enough that he secured one of the most coveted summer internships available: a position with PepsiCo, where his distinguished work caught the eye of corporate giant General Mills. They hired him for his first job out of business school.

Mark's preaching of the Good Lord's word fell by the wayside in relatively short order. He seemed to lose his religious bearings at Cambridge, a fact that did not go unnoticed by his wife, Susi. Tension between the two was inevitable. While Susi continued a life of reverence, Mark started drinking occasionally—mostly in social settings. The abrupt change in lifestyle astonished old friends like Chris Launius, who also entered the corporate world after college. Mark was now a detriment, at least to Nazarene society, and while he still remained involved in the church in body, if not wholly in spirit, this seemed to be more to oblige Susi than out of his own genuine belief. He volunteered to lead small-group ministries and served for a time on the local church board, where he lent his financial experience to good effect.

Mark's transition was no doubt smoothed over by the fact that, at the time, personal histories could not be checked with a simple Google search. It was not as if Susi would drop Mark's past into casual conversation. No one from Harvard Business School knew Mark had been a prime suspect in a savage murder, and who would think to guess? He could present, or omit, any part of his history he chose, and no one would be the wiser. Back in Olathe, of course, Mark had no control over what people thought. He acquired the nickname of "The Mangler." As in, "When are they ever going to charge The Mangler?" Or, "I heard The Mangler was at Stanford or Harvard or Yale." And finally, "The Mangler is free as a bird because the investigation is longer dead than David Harmon."

Which it was. The police had kept tabs on Mark and Melinda's mail for a while to see if they were communicating. When it became obvious they weren't, the case stopped cold. The investigation had been a board-certified disaster. If Harvard Business School examined case studies on how *not* to do things, the investigation into David Harmon's death could be considered fodder. If only the police had gotten Melinda alone or had had the fortitude to press her with Lambert in the room. Likewise, the search for the murder weapon was either unlucky or haphazard. And perhaps they should have pressured Fred Jones, who had acted as Mark's first lawyer. He was a civilian. Did he really have attorney-client privilege?

In April 1983, over a year after the murder, an editorial in the *Olathe Daily News* touched upon the local sentiment of recrimination: "The suspicion, rumor, and innuendo continue to cross this community with every day that the Olathe police say less and less about the February 28 murder of David Harmon," the article began, "This talk itself is murderous," it added. The article then defended the actions of the police and attempted to deflect any blame on the church. The last line read, "It never hurts to be patient."

Any new evidence that floated up was of sparing use, if any. The *Daily News* soon received a letter about "the conspiracy" to shut down the police investigation, along with a poem that was quickly turned over to police:

> *Pore Davey's Daid.*
>
> *Pore Davey's daid.*
> *Asleep in his bed*
> *His hair was bashed in a bloody manner.*
> *Could have been down with a ball peen hammer*
> *Whoever swung it sure ain't in no slammer.*
> *So pore Davey's daid.*
> *So pore Davey's daid.*
> *The police, they came at a lively gait*
> *And ran right in to some well laid bait*
> *W'ile the big bank changed*
> *The locks on its gate.*
> *Still pore Davey's daid.*
> *Somehow our town ain't so purty no more*
> *The folks here 'bout done shut down their roar.*

The poem was stuffed in the evidence box, which had been effectively freeze-dried on a shelf.

Even with the evidence packed away, perhaps it's no surprise that, despite numerous invitations from his friend Chris Launius to return for MNC homecomings, Mark never went back to Olathe. He would see Launius elsewhere, but never in Olathe. Harvard was his future. The past was just that.

* * * *

After David's funeral, Melinda Harmon, widow, was whisked out of Olathe on a missionary trip—to where exactly is lost to memory. Some say Africa, some say somewhere closer to home in the Midwest. She never did return to Kansas either. Her parents were by that point settled in the Columbus, Ohio area, where her father was eventually anointed a superintendent emeritus of the Nazarene Church, gaining top standing in the eyes of every Nazarene churchyard in the nation. Melinda moved into her parents' house. For a short time, she was too terrified to leave her home, though she would not say why. She received visits from a few Olathe friends, women she knew from church basement socials. Others wrote her letters. To the visitors, she seemed as depressed as any widow might, shuffling around her parents' home, either unwilling or unable to speak about David. Given openings, she all but plugged her ears.

Lacking the accountability and direction of a married Nazarene woman, Melinda began attending Ohio State University. In terms of the future, Melinda's lack of a college degree had always been a sore point for her. Part of her disillusionment with life back in Kansas, friends observed, was her frustration at being around so many people who were getting their college degrees while she had a mere certification in secretarial duties.

The grand anonymity of the largest four-year campus in the nation, Ohio State, was the perfect setting for a woman aiming to both blend in and unburden herself from the past. In this regard, Mark and Melinda were polar opposites. At every turn in life, Mark took the opportunity to stand out, to call attention to himself, and excel. Melinda only wanted to be, in the overall scheme of things, forgotten.

Even so, she was still able to leave a special impression on men. In less than two years she was engaged again, to a man who would eventually become a high-school principal in Ohio. Her alliance to the church was still so strong that, even though married once before and obviously not a virgin, Melinda would not have intercourse with her fiancée.

When the future principal found her too tempestuous and feared he was making the mistake of his life, he called off the wedding by phone. Melinda, now a student well on her way to graduation, paid him a nighttime visit and, with her mother waiting in the car, pounded on his locked apartment door. Then she went back outside and beeped the horn until the police were called and Melinda melted back into the night, leaving behind a smashed headlight.

And that's right about when—as Melinda herself would say many times—God brought her Mark. This was not Mark Mangelsdorf, who was preparing to make his mark on corporate America far from the Rust Belt of Ohio. This was Mark Raisch, a promising young dental student with an intense gaze, pockmarked skin, a soft voice, and a faultless devotion to the church.

Melinda and Mark were married on September 17, 1986, with Melinda radiant once again. Within a few years, the couple had two children, a boy, Landon, and a girl, Layne.

While the two were devout, their existence was not spartan. Mark Raisch soon had a thriving cosmetic dentistry practice. Melinda's nervous mannerisms and judgmental nature were still shortcomings, but her maternal devotion was pure. She did her best to drive her children to great heights, whether in church plays, tennis, or swimming, and maintained an active role in the PTA. She consumed herself with directing the children's church Christmas pageants. Her ardent hope was that Landon would one day go to dental school, inheriting Mark's practice (where Melinda worked part-time, alongside her mother, as a secretary).

Within a short span of time, Melinda had rebounded completely from her old life with David Harmon, a name unfamiliar to her new friends and neighbors. She was now well-cared for, well-regarded in her church, and unnoticed by the world at large. She had achieved her great goal—a total, and fairly gilded, equilibrium.

* * * *

In the days John and Sue Harmon spent in Olathe following David's death, they stayed at V.H. Lewis's home, as well as with other Lambert cousins. They were never alone with Melinda, and they were not invited to Lambert family meetings, which left John with a smoldering feeling of exclusion. When John asked for a tour of the murder scene, LaRue and other detectives described to him in detail what they thought had happened. David's killers were hiding in plain sight. The facts were in order, but no charges were meted out. The message John

Harmon heard was that he shouldn't talk about the case to anyone, even to friends, under any circumstances. Authorities in Kansas deny that this ever could have happened, but John swears he was told by District Attorney Dennis Moore and more than one detective as he left Olathe not to speak about the case with anyone in any way, shape, or form. Was there concern he'd bellyache to the media about the lack of progress? The police were already under public pressure. Were the police worried that John would compromise the investigation from his residence in Chili? It was nearly impossible to keep secrets in Olathe, and not only on big-ticket events like this one. Everyone knew everyone's business, and everyone certainly already knew the details of this case. Regardless, the request (or warning), whatever its precise intention, suited the Harmons surprisingly well.

A common occurrence in similar circumstances is that the family of the victim, enraged by the threadbare efforts of the authorities to solve the murder of their loved one, takes it upon themselves to push the buttons of justice. The Harmons however, were a kind couple who held deference for authority and were not prone to debate, especially when they were operating under what they took to be a gag order. So when John and Sue initially returned to Chili, they spoke to no one about the details of the crime. They called Kansas less than once a week to ask about progress. Over the next couple of years, the weekly calls became a call every three months. And then every four. John has no memory of when it became twice a year and does not like thinking back to that point in time when—he can't remember when, precisely—they had endured enough polite brush-offs and stopped calling altogether.

Over the years, John managed to take solace in his students. Adorning the walls of the Harmon kitchen and stretching out into the family room were the portraits of the Harmons' honorary grandchildren, students, and children of church members who would come to visit, little boys and girls who even as they grew big always made time to come over to the Harmons at Easter for an egg hunt or at Christmas to unwrap presents. To this day, John can rattle off the names of students who long ago passed to adulthood. There was Craig and his sister Merry; Tim and Dawn Iulg, who were from a Norwegian family; and a family of four bouncing children who came many times to fill their house with crumbs and laughter—Lisa, Angela, Denny, and the last, a pretty girl whose name John often trips over: Melinda, *no*, Melissa.

* * * *

Whether Mark was miraculously drawn to a life of redemption after what happened in Kansas, or whether he was just playacting his decency, knowing he could ultimately be brought before a judge or parole board, Mark's rise to power was by all counts a beneficent one.

Mark's college buddy, Chris Launius, was engaged in a more traditional climb up the corporate ladder, which is to say a tediously slow one of grinding disappointment. Job promotions were hard to come by and he harbored dreams of ditching it all for the seminary (which he eventually did). Mark had eclipsed him by a long shot, rising to the level of vice president at Pepsi nearly overnight—his first sizeable appointments were vice president of customer development and vice president and general manager of the Portland Marketing Unit in Oregon. In the words of Mark's supervisor, Keith Reimer (who later became president and COO of Pepsi Bottling Ventures), both roles had "significant leadership, P&L, and organizational impact."

Mark's mission, of course, had changed from persuading non-believers to follow Christ to persuading Coke drinkers to switch brands. He approached his job with a certain levity that surprised Launius. That wasn't the case at home, though. Once when Launius and his family were visiting, he was disturbed to witness Mark speaking to Susi in, if not quite a cutting tone, an oddly dismissive way. On one occasion, Susi was cataloguing her recent participation in church events. Whereas Mark would have once responded with a series of compliments, instead he replied with a snarky, "That's *some* use of your time."

Launius had no reference point for his friend's behavior, only the realization that Mark had changed, inexorably, at Harvard. It was not as if his friend had taken on completely contemptuous airs, though he had accumulated at least some of the arrogance that Chris seemed to think was in no short supply in large cities like Boston, New York, or even Seattle. Maybe, he thought, Mark had simply grown bored with his religion and would eventually come back into the fold. Or maybe Mark had given up trying to perfect himself. The visit marked the end of the Mangelsdorf-Launius family friendship. Mark and Launius would meet up by themselves while traveling on business within a rental car drive of each other, provided, of course, that doing so did not involve entering the city limits of Olathe.

When Mark was made general manager of the Pepsi manufacturing facility in Portland, he and Susi packed up and moved to Oregon with their two young daughters, Julia and Emily.

Mark applied the principles of equality, reason, and discipline to his business life and was known for genuinely trying to enhance the lives of others. He was ranked as the very best boss his secretary, Nicole Ritz, had ever had. Others at the company would say "If you cut me, I bleed Pepsi," but Mark had a different take and a humanity to his business practices. During a rare Oregon snowstorm with blinding conditions, Mark called almost every employee in the vast facility personally to tell them to stay home for their safety.

"We only make sticky water," he had said.

A truck driver on Mark's large staff, already on his rounds, collided with a car that had stalled on the freeway. It was an unavoidable and minor accident, but a review board held the unfortunate truck driver responsible and recommended a two-week suspension. Mark overturned the decision.

Like many corporate behemoths in the nineties, Pepsi was taking advantage of the chance to cut costs by entering into service contracts with outside national suppliers, including a janitorial service. Unfortunately, the company employed a man who, though a contract worker, had worked in the facility for years and was accepted as a member of the corporate family. He was hard working and honest enough to pick up change dropped on the floor and place it back on someone's desk. The arrangement with him, though, came to be seen as a substandard agreement—too slow, expensive, and unprofessional.

When the regional supply manager tried to scuttle the man's contract and sign one with a large national janitorial service, Mark spent political capital at Pepsi on what looked to be the very definition of a thankless task, defending the janitor against company direction. Mark saved the old man's job and rose higher still in the estimation of his co-workers.

Mark was headed toward the higher echelons of power but was never greedy—quite the opposite. He and his daughters were mentioned in *The Oregonian* in an article on serving turkey to the homeless for Christmas. When his secretary asked about it, Mark said that the girls had enough toys and that he wanted them to have a meaning-filled Christmas, not the crass modern type. Mark was not outwardly religious, Ritz knew, but he seemed steeped in the best of religious thought.

Share and share alike might have been Mark's informal motto. When the company enjoyed a particularly good year, the powers that be flew Mark and his underlings to Palm Springs for a blowout celebration. Mark included not only Ritz but her husband, Ken. And though the more casual hippie pair was intimidated by the opulence and proximity to powerful company executives, Mark went out of his way to put the couple at ease, even deferring to Ken in picking the wine at dinner.

The Palm Springs junket was indicative of Mark's growing stature, and he was soon given a plum task for which many had been angling. For his operational and marketing excellence, Mark was named general manager of Pepsi's highly promising joint venture with one of the fastest growing companies in America in 1996, Starbucks. The coffeehouse with ambitions to put a store on every block in America and the iconic American soda company created the North American Coffee Partnership. The goal was to use Starbucks' expertise in coffee, Pepsi's powerful distribution through its famed bottlers, and a dairy co-op to produce a bottled coffee drink that would be available in every grocery store in the land.

The product would be one of Mark's crowning achievements, a beverage that you see today in that short, stout bottle in stores across America. But it turned out to be no easy hill to climb.

Mark had many constituencies to satisfy, and two disparate corporate cultures to bridge—one young and aggressive, the other established and conservative. They were as far apart as Kansas and Harvard, but Mark started off with an act that received appreciative notice all around. Mark voluntarily moved to Seattle, offering to work out of Starbucks headquarters. He brought his family of five—including a son, Steven, born three years earlier, who everyone said was the spitting image of his father.

Mark earned trust from the upstart coffee company, and that gratitude helped make the North American Coffee Partnership a wild success on the nation's grocery shelves.

Mark's performance was so notable it was showcased in the book *Pour Your Heart into It*, written by Howard Schultz, the chairman and CEO of Starbucks. Schultz recounted how the first product created by the joint venture was a miserable failure. It was a lightly carbonated coffee drink called *Mazagran*, a name borrowed from the French

This chapel steeple has been atop The College Church of the Nazarene since 1968.
It catches light from the Olathe sky, reflecting different moods depending upon the
weather and angle of the sun.

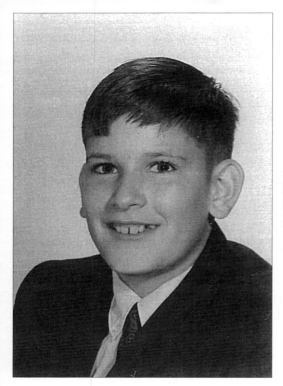

As a boy, David Harmon was known for his size and quiet nature, as well as for h knack for sketching buildings and memo rizing Bible verses.

David Harmon's 1975 senior high school yearbook photo.

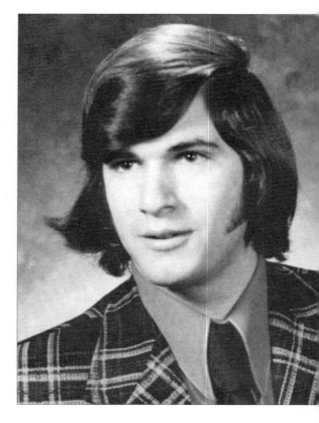

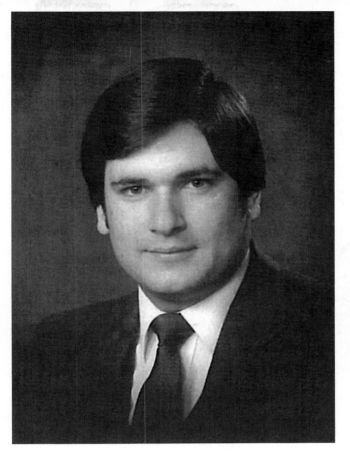

David Harmon in a photo taken when he was in his early twenties and living in Olathe, Kansas.

Mark Mangelsdorf in a MidAmerica Nazarene yearbook photo. Mark was student body president, staged Christian rock concerts, and received an award granted to the graduating senior who best exemplified the work of Jesus Christ.

linda Harmon, who worked as the dean's secretary, as pictured he MidAmerica Nazarene yearbook.

The Harmon/Bergstrand duplex in the winter of 1982. The Harmons lived on the right and the Bergstrands lived on the left. More than an hour after the murder, Melinda ran next door, oddly composed.

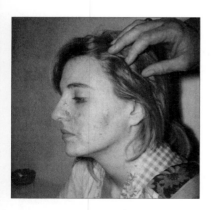

Melinda Harmon with her lightly bruised check.

The brute force of the blows inflicted on David Harmon as he slept was enough to splatter blood across the Harmons' bedroom clear onto the opposite wall.

Splattered blood on a wedding photo of David and Melinda Harmon. The two met as teenagers at a Bible camp in New York and married at twenty, before making a life for themselves in Kansas, where many of their fellow evangelicals were settling.

Melinda Raisch's home as seen by a surveillance photo taken by Ohio police on behalf of Olathe detectives, to prepare them for their surprise visit. The detectives wanted to make certain that Melinda's father, who lived nearby, was nowhere in sight when they knocked on the door.

Until his sentencing in 2006, Mark Mangelsdorf lived comfortably in this house in the well-heeled suburb of Pelham, NY, with his second wife, Kristina, a top official at PepsiCo.

Mark and a pregnant Kristina in the doorway of their sitting room in the fall of 2005. At first, Kristina, tired after a long day of work, did not want to be photographed—but envisioning what it would look like for Mark to be standing alone, she relented.

Mark Mangelsdorf and his wife Kristina were surrounded by media in February of 2006 as they left the Johnson County Courthouse after Mark pleaded guilty to second-degree murder.

John Harmon at Mark's sentencing, a day he waited twenty-four years for.

Mark listens to John Harmon's anguished statement at his sentencing, flanked by his lawyers, Scott Kreamer (to Mark's right), scion of a powerful Kansas legal family, and Michael (Mickey) Sherman (to Mark's left), who also defended Kennedy cousin Michael Skakel in a cold murder case.

Kristina sits watching Mark's sentencing. She alternately held strong and dissolved to tears. Seated beside her is her mother, Susan Friberg.

Melinda Raisch at her sentencing. Tom Bath, one of her lawyers and a man often in the thick of murder cases involving the privileged in Kansas, stands to her left. Ran Austin, another lawyer who returned to legal service from managing a real estate inheritance in order to defend Melinda, stands to her right.

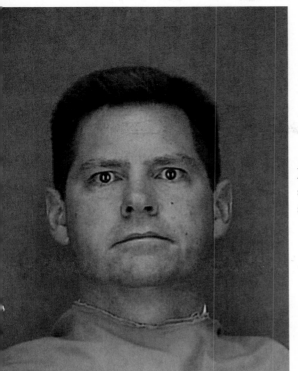

Mark's mug shot, soon after sentencing. He looked fraught and uncharacteristically uncertain.

Melinda's mug shot, soon after sentencing. Authorities laughed that it looked like a glamour shot.

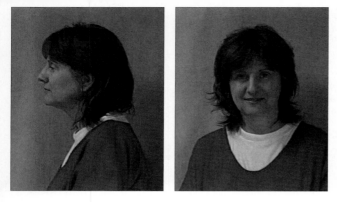

Melinda's mugshot from the Kansas Department of Correct[...]
Always smiling, she invested i[...]
presenting a good front.

Detectives Bill Wall and Steve James, the partners who were asked by a regional crime lab official in 2001 if there were any cold cases in need of a fresh look. They reopened the Harmon case, which had been abandoned in storage.

Paul Morrison at a press conference in Topeka, Kansas, in early 2008. Morrison's first murder scene as an assistant district attorney was David Harmon's and the sight made him queasy. Two decades later, by the time the last threads of the Harmon case came together, Morrison was running for Kansas attorney general.

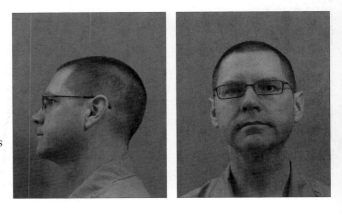

rk's mugshots from the Kansas partment of Corrections. this time, he had adjusted to surroundings.

David Harmon's grave in Olathe, Kansas. A fellow church member offered to finance the digging up of David's body, in order to move him closer to the upstate New York home of David's parents, John and Sue, who, with limited means, went twenty years without visiting the grave of their only child. John declined the offer, saying that David had lived his life right by Jesus and should rest where he was.

Foreign Legion posted in Algeria during the nineteenth century. It was only when the *frappuccino* hit Starbucks stores and Pepsi found a shelf-safe way to get it into bottles that beverage history was made— thanks in large part to Mark, who was before too long named head of marketing for the Pepsi Bottling Company.

Susi had, in the interim, worked toward a Masters in social work. Though she did not work when her children were young, becoming a therapist had always been Susi's dream. The fading of Mark's religious beliefs, though, caused irreparable damage to their marriage, and by the mid 1990s they reached a point of impasse. Mark and Susi were officially divorced in 1997.

Around the time of his divorce, Mark supervised Kristina Friberg, a fellow rider on the soft drink fast track who would eventually become the head of marketing for Pepsi's diet beverage division. The product of a European boarding school, a Harvard education, and an MBA from the University of Virginia, Friberg was the daughter of Eric Friberg, director emeritus of McKinsey and Co., a well regarded global consulting firm; a top player in leveraged buyouts as a senior advisor with Kohlberg, Kravis and Roberts; and the board chairman of the School of Business at William and Mary. Kristina was being transferred to New York, but Mark missed her going-away party because he had gone to see the movie *Titanic* instead. He called with an apology and the suggestion that he take her out to dinner to make it up to her.

The two began dating, and Mark soon moved to New York himself for a short time to take up his marketing post at Pepsi Bottling. On one of their first dates, they closed down a Mediterranean restaurant on the

Upper West Side of Manhattan, having one of those epic conversations a couple has early on in their relationship when they are laying it all bare, sharing their dark secrets. Kristina told Mark about how once, traveling in Spain, she was almost raped.

In return, Mark spoke about his best friend's brutal murder, and the moral laxity and incompetence of the police that led to him being treated as a suspect. Rather than recoiling, Kristina was intrigued. Throughout her life, her book shelves had been filled with mysteries and thrillers, from Nancy Drew (as an adult she kept her set in immaculate condition) to John Grisham.

Kristina asked Mark a series of questions, eager to try and solve the murder that very night. The killer couldn't have been Mark, obviously, but who had it been? They left the restaurant with the workers cleaning up around their feet and no suspect either of them could pinpoint.

In 1999, the couple was married at the Cathedral of St. Philip, a beautiful Episcopal church on Peachtree Road in the Buckhead section of Atlanta. St. Philip was a spiritual reference point for Kristina's parents. Even when they moved from Atlanta to their dream retirement community in Charleston, South Carolina, where they became valued patrons of historical preservation charities, St. Philip would be a touchstone for them. The subdued worship in the pews at St. Philip could not have been a greater counterpoint to the amen-energy of the Nazarene College Church. Kristina was less devout than her parents, but pleased to have a wedding at St. Philip, which she had dreamed of since she was young.

The ceremony, which attracted local society, coincided with Mark's decision, lured by the apparently easy money of the Internet boom, to ditch Pepsi, leveraging his prominent success with the Starbucks endeavor to take a top position and a boat load of stock options from Webvan, an online grocery concern. He would run Webvan's entire region in the Dallas area. Kristina secured a sought-after post with Frito-Lay, a Pepsi subsidiary, and the two made their home in Plano, in a neighborhood where a number of the Dallas Cowboy players lived.

Mark was right that online delivery of groceries had potential, but he was early by the better part of a decade. FreshDirect would later become what he thought Webvan would be, though Webvan's bankruptcy in 2001 came through no fault of his strategies. When Webvan went belly up, Mark's potentially lucrative options were lost in the ether. Like any corporate survivor worth his salt, Mark soon landed in a better spot. He was named chief operating officer of Omni Services, which generated well over $300 million in revenues as the nation's second most successful uniform renter. The company was so impressed with Mark's organizational brilliance and adept sales instincts that it was willing to overlook the not insignificant factor that Mark had no experience with uniforms.

Mark settled into his rewarding new role at Omni (the office was in Culpeper, Virginia; he commuted home to Plano on weekends by plane). The job was another impressive corporate feather in his cap.

Then Mark, like Melinda, answered a knock at the door.

FIVE

The revival of the investigation started on little more than a lark.

In August 2001, a woman from the Johnson County crime lab came out to Olathe to ask if they happened to have any cold cases. Legend around the police station held that if ever there were a case that needed resuscitating—with a little help from a modern forensic specialist and God—it was David Harmon's murder. Since the torrential flood that had soaked the case file, there had been little, if any, progress. It had been years since John and Sue Harmon had called asking for the slightest update and, without their push to roust anyone, time and inertia had taken their toll. The joke was that the only way to get put in charge of the Harmon case was to ask.

The man who finally did the asking was Olathe Police Department Detective Bill Wall. Taking over the Harmon case was not the self-destructive career move it appeared to be on the surface. Since the original investigation was not his mishap, what did he have to lose? Wall asked his supervisor, Sergeant Steve James, to reopen the case, and together they lobbied their commander, Mel Richie, for the chance to revive the investigation in its entirety and—here was the showstopper—for a budget to follow through on any and all leads. Wall and James both admired Roger LaRue, now retired. LaRue had been their mentor. If they could resurrect this case, and solve it, it would be as much for his sake as for theirs.

Ever since Wall had joined the Olathe Police Department as a patrol officer, he'd heard snippets here and there about the Harmon case from Roger and the older detectives. He heard how the Nazarenes had amassed enough power to squelch the thing and Wall, as much as he loved Roger, could not fathom how he could have let any organization obstruct a murder investigation. But it was Wall, Roger explained, who couldn't fathom the political pressure coming from Dennis Moore, the district attorney. This is what hamstrung the Harmon case. It was not as if the DA wished for anyone to get away with murder. But the other detectives were unanimous in thinking that Moore, politically ambitious (and soon to be elected to Congress), did not want to go out on a limb to anger the Nazarene Church.

Wall thought he'd have better luck this time around. He had a reputation within the department for being able to elicit confessions like no one else.

To Wall and James's considerable surprise, they were granted a larger budget than they ever expected, one that allowed for both DNA testing and extensive travel. In terms of DNA, their base of information was almost nil. The only reliable blood testing available at the time of the murder was for type, slight by modern standards. What's more, samples cannot be preserved forever. Blood degrades—we do return to dust, despite the rigorous efforts of science. There was no telling how decipherable any of the blood evidence would prove.

Wall and James were making the fair assumption from the blood type and their best hunches that all the blood samples were David's. The attack was not the sort of scratch and claw struggle that would leave both attacker and victim wounded, with their DNA mixed. In the cold calculation of investigators, such murders are ideal.

In this case, though, the blood evidence would probably illustrate what they already knew, which was also what the detectives of nineteen years earlier suspected, but had been unable to prove. Melinda's home-invasion testimony was transparently false. David's blood was on her pillow, but not on her own head, which meant she had not been sleeping, as she claimed, at the moment the chilling blows crushed her husband's skull. There was also blood spattered on the lower portion of her nightgown, indicating that instead of being jolted awake by the attack and running away, Melinda instead stood at a moderate distance and watched as her husband was bludgeoned to death.

More blood—presumably David's—had been found on the lower reaches of the shower curtain. Someone had been hell bent on cleaning up after the murder, but had missed some traces. Blood had also been found in Mark's apartment, on a swatch of carpet, and, curiously, inside his vacuum cleaner. Cumulatively this evidence had the potential to be damning but was a long way from proving the case beyond a reasonable doubt. Even if all the results came back positive, which was doubtful, the evidence would be more incriminating for Melinda than for Mark—she was the only one who could definitely be placed at the murder scene.

The advanced DNA tests that could peg what blood sample belonged to whom with near mathematical certainty could take anywhere from several weeks to several months. Wall and James were concerned that if they waited for the results, someone with a distant connection to the church would tip off Mark and Melinda to the fact that the case had been re-opened. So without any conclusive DNA evidence, a murder weapon, or even a single witness, Wall and James decided to forge ahead.

All they had was the element of surprise.

* * * *

Now officially the first new players in the investigation since the Reagan era, Wall and James went over the case file folder by folder until they felt like putting wash rags on their eyes. They then spoke to Paul Morrison. He had been an assistant district attorney at the time. The Harmon apartment was Paul's first murder scene, and he had always promised to do something to solve the mystery when he had the chance. Now he was a popular district attorney, a dozen years into office. Morrison, in the midst of striving for higher political ambitions, never did get around to doing that "something." Now was his chance. He pledged his unwavering support.

Wall and James's first stop was a Sunday dinner at the Harmon home in Chili. James felt it was crucial to find out as much as they could to help bring the corpse to life in the courtroom. Here, the key would be to listen—which, as Wall was the first to admit, was a skill with which he had trouble. Wall had a gift for gab and James's quiet nature meant Wall could take the lead with his blessing. There was no hierarchy here.

Wall and James did not go to the Harmons to goad them into talking about any particular piece of evidence—they knew that the old couple did not know much more than they did—but as a starting point, the Harmons seemed as good as any. There was a distant chance that there would be insights, a sudden memory of ill-conduct on Melinda's part that would magically put her role in the crime in a revealing new light.

Having an investigative file in an old murder case that reads like an obituary page hampers any investigation. Here the roster of the living, at this stage in the investigation, did as much good as the dead. David's father, John, told Wall and James what he could about David and his memories of the old investigators like LaRue, while Sue displayed the family photos, pointing out how she had torn Melinda from her scrapbooks. There was, however, no magic in Chili, no case-closing revelation. Beyond the fruitless trip to the Harmons, Wall and James did not want to start contacting old witnesses for fear word in the still-tight knit community of Nazarenes would leak back to Mark and Melinda. The only way to prevent that was to confront the suspects directly.

Deciding to drop in on Melinda first was an intuitive decision, really, no better than a hunch. Mark, given his Harvard MBA and subsequent accomplishments, was probably a tactician who wouldn't scare easily. Wall and James also assumed he wouldn't make the gross miscalculation that stood as their major hope—spouting off details about the case without asking for a lawyer.

Melinda seemed the better bet. From the looks of the files, Melinda probably would have told all in the days after David's murder if Lambert had not been allowed to run the show. Perhaps she had grown remorseful over time. Wall felt that because the murder victim was her husband, maybe at some level she needed to clear her conscience.

It was anyone's guess, but both Wall and James agreed that Mark's conscience would be pretty complacent.

* * * *

In the privacy of her ornate, double-height foyer, Melinda Raisch— wearing a bathrobe, her hair wrapped just-so in the spiral of a bath towel—listened as Detective Wall, standing with Detective James and Eric Griffin, said, "We came to talk to you about the murder of your husband, David. We've reopened the case and we're hoping you can help us."

Wall tried to sound neutral, even sympathetic, to pull her into the fold. While interviewing a suspect—something Wall did with a greater rate of success than anyone Olathe had ever seen—he always had to be thinking and adapting. Like all businesses, his was a cold-blooded one, composed of little more than tactics and strategies that had to be crafted, then constantly reassessed. With luck, in the end, you won out with a confession. Most times you got heated denials or blank stares.

"Step right this way," Melinda said. "Care for coffee? I'll make a fresh pot."

"If we could sit down with you, that'd be great," Wall replied. "Do you want to take a moment to get yourself changed?" She could not be questioned only one hand grip from being naked.

"Sure," said Melinda, her tone matter-of-fact, curt.

"We'll wait here," Wall said, as Melinda turned and walked up the stairs.

The phone rang. Melinda picked up after a single ring. If she picked up that fast, she must be jumpy. Who could be on the other end? Was the caller offering a warning about a couple of Kansas detectives snooping around? Besides asking Griffin to case the house, Wall and James had done hardly any background work in order to maintain the element of surprise. They knew the arms of the Nazarene community in Olathe were long and stretched back to Ohio.

The house, as they expected, seemed empty but for Melinda upstairs. Crosses, inspirationals, and ornate religious-themed decorations were set about with precision. The bedroom was well out of earshot, too far away for them to tell if she was off the phone yet, their overriding concern. What was taking her so long? Wall envisioned her coming down and saying, "Sorry, that was my father. I can't talk to you now. Or ever."

Yet she soon returned, dressed in blue sweat pants and a white Gap sweatshirt. She had brushed her hair.

Melinda showed them to the kitchen table, sitting at the head. Wall sat next to her, James on her other side, Eric one person removed. In this light, the toll that time had taken on Melinda was clear. Her face, compared to the suggestive young woman of the file photos of years ago, had been ravaged by age. Or guilt.

Wall started over, asking for her help.

"I don't know how I can help," she replied. Wall said that they had new DNA evidence and were close to breaking the case. This was an exaggeration, but as he spoke he did his best to size Melinda up. Wall thought she could best be described as unflinching. Melinda had a knack for religious conformity, and a way of shaking her head in disapproval at those not willing to seek out the promise of better days with Jesus by their side. She could quote scripture in her sleep, or patiently wage a war of attrition on a lost soul. She hadn't, after all, blurted out a conscience-clearing confession at the front door. The key was whether Melinda, who was about their age, had been taken unaware by their arrival or had been, on some primitive level, expecting them for years, strangers from an official world far removed from her life of evangelical Christianity. In truth, Wall was pleased Melinda hadn't told them all to get lost.

"And you were there that night," Wall continued after a long pause. "What do you remember about the case?"

"Well," Melinda said, looking down, "I remember that night seeing a man, a shadowy figure hitting David. I ran to the bathroom and then downstairs. And the man came down. And it was dark. He was in the living room. He was wearing a homemade cloth mask."

Wall had to stop himself from sliding off the chair. Without any prompting beyond a simple, open-ended question, the pair of black guys was out in favor of one man and a cloth mask. It was inconceivable. Had Melinda forgotten her cover story? Or had she just decided to tell the God's honest truth? And if so, why did it take so little? If Roger

LaRue and the boys had gotten her away from her cursing, threatening father, could they have done this nineteen years ago?

Wall and James had to stop themselves from making eye contact, which might break the spell. Even Eric, who knew only the rough outline of the case, was astounded but kept his composure.

Wall, handed the option on a platter, confronted her with the discrepancy. Forget Wall the master interrogator. A kindergarten finger painter could have run this show.

"You seem to be remembering it a little differently than back in 1982," he said. "Did you lie then?"

She hadn't lied, Melinda said, she was just frightened. Frightened for her life. "But I have a feeling, a feeling in my heart that this it how it happened."

This set a pattern for the next two hours, where everything would be a "feeling" and nothing a fact. To lead off, for whatever reason, with such apparent candor and then bob and weave, hinting that there was more, led Wall to believe they were dealing with a weird bird. At several points, when an apparent impasse had been reached and the repetition got almost comical, Wall and James pushed out their chairs, an affectation meant to force Melinda into a corner. They were leaving, Wall said, to talk to neighbors, school officials, and customers of her husband's dental practice.

"We didn't come to Ohio for nothing," he said. "We're going to do plenty of background. And that's what you do when you do background—you talk to neighbors. And we're going to check with the children' attendance office, to make sure they haven't been absent too much. To check for domestic abuse."

Melinda's hand rose in protest each time.

"No," she said, "don't go. I want to help. Tell me how I can help you."

Wall said, "All you can tell us is the truth, and if the truth hurts you, so be it."

Whereupon Melinda would dish out another small tidbit, like about her emotionally inappropriate relationship with Mark. Wall brought up the letters, but she was adamant that there was no sex, that it was an unconsummated—though inappropriate—relationship. Wall did not doubt that. Melinda said that there was never any intercourse even when she was engaged to David, just heavy petting and oral sex. A lack of sex in this repressed religious environment—and the tantalizing prospect of it—might have laid siege to young Mangelsdorf.

"You must have killed your husband, then," Wall said. "Either you or Mark, or both, working together."

"I can tell you this. I did not kill my husband."

Did Mark? she was asked repeatedly.

Melinda would fall silent, but never become overly emotional. Wall found Melinda strangely malleable and yet equally manipulative. He also had a close shave with a colossal error, telling her he wanted her to be on "the right side of the investigation," in response to her wanting him to be her advocate. Despite Wall's attempts at a repair job—defining "advocate" every which way but the one that would get the interview in legal trouble—she would not let the concept go.

The detectives were interrupted by another phone call and a deliveryman. Both the phone and the doorbell gave the detectives a hundred heart attacks apiece. At one point Wall pulled out the manila crime scene photos, a gallery of images guaranteed to give even someone who had not been married to David wakeful nights. Melinda turned her head and shoved her chair back as if bitten.

Wall told her that the investigation was going forward and unless she got on the right side of the investigation, she'd never see her children again.

Melinda sat with her face in her hands, silent for what seemed to be minutes.

"I was woken up by thuds," she said finally, "and I shot up and ran to the bathroom. And I was frightened and scared and terrified so I froze in there. Then I decided to run downstairs. And soon I saw a shadowy figure of a man, with some type of homemade cloth mask."

Then she added, "And I knew in my heart that it was Mark."

Without a tape or video recorder, he had to get her to the local sheriff's department to revive their discussion there. He discussed this with Melinda and—to his surprise—she was more than willing. She just had to make new car pool arrangements for piano and tennis practice for her son and daughter—who were eleven and seven years old. She went to the downstairs bathroom, and then came directly back.

"I wish I had something to feed you all," she said.

It must have been a lonely ride to the sheriff's department for Melinda, who sat in the front seat and said nothing. Wall and James, in the back seat, only once risked eye contact.

In the interrogation room, Melinda made a phone call, saying she was tied up with something and would be done shortly.

Wall's conversation with Melinda in the interrogation room started along the same course as it had at Melinda's house.

"But, the more I absorb this, okay," she said, "what I told you back at the house is how I really sense things happened."

She was deluding herself, alternately reliving 1982 and detaching herself from what was going on in the present.

Wall mentioned Melinda's technically chaste relationship with Mark.

"David would not have approved. Is that fair?"

"We flirted in a way we should not have," Melinda answered.

"That would explain the letters," he said.

She mentioned that Mark had somehow signaled to her that something unmentionably bad might befall her husband. "I feel terrible for saying that," she said, "because it makes it seem as if I didn't stop something bad from happening."

"There are only two people who could have killed him," Wall said.

"Well it wasn't me. Let me get that clear right now."

"All right. If you say you didn't kill him, who did?"

"Well, I know in my heart it was Mark."

Wall bore in on the glaring inconsistency with her earlier accounts, saying that she must have been protecting Mark because she had played a role in the murder and wanted her husband dead.

"Well I guess you say things out of protection," she added, not mentioning whether she was protecting herself, Mark, or both. "In my heart, I always knew it was him."

"Why didn't you ever tell the real story?" Wall asked.

"It was a sense of horror to me to ever think about it or go there, okay?"

"You didn't want to deal?"

"Right, because my hands were full dealing with grief and a new life and trying to make sense of life in general."

"Mark Mangelsdorf was pretending to be David's friend while romancing his wife and planning to kill him," Wall said. "But that was going on and you knew about it and you weren't doing anything about it?"

"Well, yeah, and that I would be blamed for not crusading more for my marriage."

"Well, that day, you must have sensed something."

"I was very confused."

"Because of the feelings you were having for your husband and this man, Mark. I think it's safe to say that you were in love with two guys at the same time."

Melinda shrugged. "Could be." She leaned forward, plaintive. "How can I help you fill in more voids here? I never not loved my husband, okay? I want to help you fill in any voids here."

"You have been living with this for a long time, and you had to get on with your life," Wall said, "and just haven't thought about it?"

"I don't mean that in a heartless way," she answered.

Melinda spoke about where she was at fault—not truncating Mark's flirtations. "But where I'm bad, where this is bad, is that I was negligent in not nipping that off. I should have said, 'Buzz off' and I'm not saying he did it without encouragement from me, because there were times that I befriended him and probably was flirtatious in a way and I shouldn't have been. So I'm not saying it was all his fault."

She repeated her calls for Wall to be her advocate, something he had to all but use the Jaws of Life to extricate himself from. He said he would call Paul Morrison to see if he couldn't get her some form of a deal.

Wall told Morrison that Melinda was actually talking—*and how*—but hadn't made a full confession yet. Morrison wasn't willing to offer a deal unless she told everything. Wall went back to talk to Melinda.

"Do you still think the truth is more important than what happens to you?" he asked.

"Yes," she said "but your humanness comes out."

"If you had knowledge," Wall began to say.

"That's the part you know, see," Melinda interrupted. "I did not have specific knowledge, but I've told you I have knowledge."

"Well, then there are no secrets."

"I had warnings I did not heed, and I'm devastated."

"So there is a little more here?"

Melinda looked at Wall. "There's a little more," she said.

There *was* more to tell, but Melinda needed a true advocate, a lawyer. "I need to know where I stand," Melinda said. Wall, drained by this point and bound by law, relented. He hoped that the conversation would be continued shortly, but that was the last Wall spoke to Melinda that day. The next morning, Wall called to say that they would not be canvassing neighbors and school board members and could they talk again today?

Melinda said most definitely not.

Wall could only guess why Melinda abruptly changed her mind. Had someone else gotten to her? It could have been one of any number of people—her father, her new husband, a lawyer. All he knew for certain was that he would be heading back to Kansas without the benefit of an explanation for Melinda's sudden reversal, or any more time to interview Melinda. Without that, there was only one person left to see.

* * * *

With Christmas coming, Mark's ambush would have to wait. Wall and James, both family men, knew that no matter what the career stakes were or how much hung in the balance in terms of justice, traveling anywhere in the vicinity of Christmas and New Year's was as good a way as any to antagonize their wives.

Wall and James were also in a bind. They had to keep a tight lid on the case, but now that they had contacted Melinda, there was a chance she would tell Mark, who could then hire a team of sterling lawyers before their investigation gained any traction.

Paul Morrison was personally taking on the prosecution of both Mark and Melinda. In an ideal world, Mark, who had probably wielded the club, was Morrison's big-ticket item, so Morrison decided to discuss a plea deal with Melinda's attorneys that would allow her to plead guilty to a lesser charge than murder—say, being an accessory to murder—in exchange for testifying against Mark and receiving a drastically reduced sentence. It would not be to Melinda's advantage, then, to give Mark an inkling of what was afoot, lest he turn on her and grab a deal first.

In mid-January 2002, after initial plea discussions with Melinda proved fruitless, Wall and James headed to Plano, Texas, opting to drive, since they had been unsettled by their post–September 11 flights to and from Ohio. This gave the Plano Police Department time to case Mark's house—just as Griffin had done in Ohio—in order to make sure he would be home when Wall and James popped out of the past.

Posing as officials from the alarm company looking to forward updated information to the local police, Wall and James found out from Kristina exactly when Mark, who at the time was commuting halfway across the country to the Virginia headquarters of Omni Services, would be home. They were not so much lying to Kristina as they were selectively informing her. Like the ruse about DNA with Melinda, such maneuvers were wholly legal. Finding out when Mark was home would, as it turned out, be the easy part. Mark, they guessed, was more worldly than Melinda, would have more psychological armature in place, and would not be as eager to please.

It was nearly 6:00 P.M. when Mark Mangelsdorf answered the knock at his door.

After their success with Melinda, Wall (with a tape recorder hidden in his sleeve) and James had a good deal more confidence. The detectives introduced themselves and Mark turned visibly stiff, rigid. Wall noticed with some glee that Mark's right hand was shaking.

"We are going to need a minute of your time," said Wall cheerfully. "Is anybody else here?"

Mark, still unnerved, shook his head no. Wall thought they were going to have to hook this guy up to a tow chain to pull him up off the floor. He told Mark they would like him to come down to the Plano Police Department so they could, in a quaint turn of phrase, "share" some new developments in the case.

"How would that be?" Wall asked.

Gathering himself, Mark answered, "Actually, I'd prefer not to do anything without a lawyer."

Mark's invoking his right to counsel, as the phrase goes, should have ended the interview. Wall, too jazzed, was only just beginning.

"Okay, well, I thought you might say that, but I think if I were you, I mean if—I would be awful curious about what's going on. We talked to Melinda. Have you talked to her lately?"

"I have not."

Wall adopted a sort of jaunty casualness in his tone. He told Mark that Melinda was living in Ohio, and tried to gauge whether Mark knew that already. He didn't appear to. Mark affected a calm, welcoming look, though considering the circumstances there was almost a hint of mockery to it.

"You . . . you haven't seen her in twenty years?" Wall asked. When Mark answered that he hadn't, Wall again asked if they could "share" some of their new developments with him.

"Still . . . still don't . . ." Mark stammered.

Advantage Wall, who smiled broadly. He had gotten one over on Mark by just showing up at his front door. "Looks like you are a little off base here. Are you caught off guard here a little bit?"

"Absolutely," said Mark, who seemed more clear-eyed upon hearing the sound of his own honest answer.

"You are probably wondering how we found you and all that kind of stuff, right?"

It was a bad question, as a simple Internet search could do the trick. "I'm not wondering that. You know, I haven't made my whereabouts hidden or anything like that," Mark replied, showing less deference.

"Have you heard anything about the case in the last twenty years?"

"No, I haven't."

"Have you been curious about what happened? James and I have been investigating this case and seems to me like you just kind of left without much being said. Is that fair?"

"You know," said Mark, "I don't want to comment on any assumptions that you are making. I have, I certainly have my perspectives and point of view, but—"

Wall saw the door beginning to open. "Well, we would love to sit down and talk to you about—"

Mark waved him off. "Based on, based on the way things were at the time, I didn't feel things were fair. The way I left it with my attorney at the time"—again, a bothersome reference to an attorney—"Hugh and Scott Kreamer asked me not to speak any further with the police about the case without having an attorney present."

"Yeah," said Wall, still on a roll, "but that was twenty years ago. We were just—we re-opened the case—you've heard of cold cases, haven't you?"

"Not really. No."

Wall briefly explained the process. "We went back and re-interviewed all the old cops that you knew probably. Do you remember any of their names?"

"I don't."

"'Roger LaRue,' does that ring a bell?"

"No."

"Well, we went back and did all that kind of stuff and now it's kind of led us back to you 'cause we wanted to get your perspective twenty years later as to what your thoughts were on all this. That's why we traveled down from Olathe today to come visit you. That's why we knocked on your door. I'm sure we caught you completely off guard and you're probably nervous about it. You probably haven't even thought about this in a long time. And that's why we'd like to invite you down to the police department. You'll drive or come in our car. You're not under arrest. We just want to share some of these things with you."

"I will not do that without an attorney," Mark said.

After more back and forth about the unsolved nature of the case, Wall asked a loaded question. "You're in sales, right?"

"No, I'm in general management. Chief Operating Officer of a company."

"Well, you have a beautiful home, that's for sure." Mark had let them into the foyer—no sign of religion here—but he had let them in only to avoid a spectacle in front of the house, not as any sort of welcome.

Kevin Grisham, the local escort, had, like James, been silent up to this point. He probably should have broken things up after Mark asked for a lawyer more times that he could count on his fingers, but now he was overwhelmed by curiosity.

"Does your wife know about this?" Grisham asked.

"Pardon, yes," Mark replied.

"Okay. She knows everything that's happened in the past?"

"Uh, well, you say *everything* that's happened in the past?"

"This case?" Grisham asked.

"She's aware of this case, yes."

"Did you ever share with her your thoughts that back then you thought they focused on you as a suspect?"

"Yes."

Conversationally, Wall, for one of the first times in his life, was flustered. He did not want to leave things on a "down" note, especially after how well the drop-in with Melinda had gone. He went on a bit about search warrants that had been served on Mark's home and car, but soon Grisham knew it was time to end what was turning into a charade. He noted Mark's request for a lawyer but asked if he'd give a mouth swab for DNA before they left.

Mark said no, and Wall was in on him again, talking about how they had traveled so far to get here. Mark replied that he had a phone and they should have called.

It was a tactic, Wall said. Didn't Mark use tactics in business?

"Uh, I certainly do."

"And I try to use those kinds of tactics too," said Wall, almost apologetically explaining too much.

No sooner had Wall said that then Kristina walked in the front door.

"Hi," she said, hospitable, but obviously puzzled.

Mark spoke up quickly. "Kristina, these folks are from the Olathe police and this gentleman is from the Plano Police Department. I'll get an attorney, but I choose not to talk to them."

"Okay," Wall said.

"Okay," Kristina repeated, "thank you."

They all exchanged business cards and brittle good-byes. Wall and James had put the thousand-yard stare into Mark.

A few days later, Wall, James, and Grisham returned, pulling into Mark's driveway just as Mark did. As Mark went to lug wine coolers out of his trunk for a party that night—Wall and James exchanging wry looks at the nice Nazarene boy who now apparently drank—he was informed they were there to obtain a DNA swab.

Getting DNA from Mark was part act of intimidation and part fishing expedition. The intimidation portion of the equation was fairly self-evident. Wall and James sensed rightly that the prospect of modern DNA testing on ancient pieces of evidence must be a source of sleepless nights for anyone who has gotten away with a murder that's been declared a "cold case." With only a small chance that a sample could tie Mark inexorably to the crime, their larger objective was surprising Mark, and unsettling him once he was surprised. There is no telling what will happen when you make an important man sweat.

Mark set down the wine coolers and said in a polite but guarded tone that he wouldn't give a sample without talking to his lawyer. Grisham told Mark that under Texas law, a warrant was all they needed and, if necessary, they could tackle him and get it that way instead. Just the same, Grisham said, as a courtesy, Mark could call his lawyer if he wanted. No need to do things the hard way here.

Mark went inside the house to call, carrying his wine coolers with him. Wall sidled up to Kristina.

"I don't know how much you know about this case," he told her, "but you need to do some research on it or something. You have to find out what he did."

"Okay," she said, refusing to engage.

Mark returned, having been unable to get through to his lawyer. Faced with the prospect of being on the wrong end of a dog pile of detectives, he allowed them to swab his mouth.

The lawyer Mark could not get through to was Scott Kreamer, the son of Hugh Kreamer, the powerful old district attorney who took Mark on as his last case. Scott was working out of a law office right down the block from the Johnson County Courthouse in Olathe, where a trial most likely would be held. Kreamer had a local practice that didn't revolve around big-ticket criminal cases (he specialized in divorces or "matrimonial law") but his firm was seen as a player in the Kansas legal community. With his Kansas contacts, Kreamer could come in handy.

Morrison, meanwhile, was taking his time in bringing charges in the case. This came both from necessity and in an attempt to turn Mark skittish. He was also limited by the evidence, which was hardly exhaustive. The swab Mark donated under threat of being pounced on did not, as expected, amount to anything. Investigators still had a fingerprint on the back patio, but Mark never disputed spending time at David and Melinda's duplex. Copious amounts of David's DNA in Mark's apartment, now confirmed with near certainty, could also be excused with a variant of the same explanation—David had been to his apartment numerous times. If Melinda caved and turned evidence,

Mark would have his first significant problem but, even there, Mark's lawyers could argue that Melinda had now told two different stories and would presumably have to tell a third.

Melinda refused to barter that third story for lenience and was indicted for murder in December 2003. Thinking better of an attempt to indict Mark at this point, considering the still circumstantial nature of the case against him, Morrison instead named Mark in Melinda's indictment as an unindicted co-conspirator, effectively placing him in a legal purgatory. Not officially accused yet publicly named, Mark remained, as he had been for years, uncharged. And yet Melinda's indictment, in the stilted, hedged voice of a legal document, brought the night of the murder, and Mark's part in it, alive after so many years of silence:

> *Mark Mangelsdorf and/or Melinda Harmon aka Melinda Raisch struck David Harmon numerous times in the head with a blunt instrument, killing him. Mark Mangelsdorf and/or Melinda Harmon aka Melinda Raisch moved the blanket covering the body of David Harmon, pulled out a drawer in the bedroom and took a lid off a dish containing keys to make it appear as though a residential robbery had occurred. . . . Mark Mangelsdorf left the above mentioned residence and disposed of the murder weapon.*

In the long lead-up to Melinda's trial, the case against Mark never did magically get better. Without Melinda's testimony, it would simply be a truncated case. If legal proceedings against Melinda unraveled in acquittal, Mark might never be formally charged. As a result, Mark took Melinda's legal fate with the utmost seriousness.

In the midst of such personal uncertainty, Mark's corporate good fortunes took yet another turn. Cintas, the nation's largest uniform renter, purchased Omni in an effort to expand cross-selling opportunities and to save costs on redundancies. Mark made millions on the deal, enough to elicit a giddy mention from Kristina in her European boarding-school alumni magazine.

After the Cintas-Omni takeover, one of the redundancies in the post was the position of chief operating officer. Mark had to take the money and run, which he did, and gladly, as he no longer had to commute by airplane. In short order, Mark was able to secure his loftiest post yet, the one that could propel him into the chief executive officer slot of a reputable multi-billion dollar multinational organization.

In 2004, Parmalat's President and CEO, Mike Rosicki, made Mark what they call in corporate work "an offer he could not refuse"—to start and run an entirely new carbonated beverage division at an international conglomerate with an uncannily long string of profitable years. Done well, it would put him in standing to be Rosicki's successor. Mark and Kristina, who now had a baby daughter, Charlotte, moved to an elegant house in Pelham, a coveted New York City suburb, in order to commute to Parmalat's stateside headquarters in Secaucus, New Jersey.

Pelham was the closest well-appointed village in the northern portion of the suburban ring around New York City, and had thus always been home to the privileged and the elite. Appearances were kept up without fail, with the town having only a limited number of predigested troubles—a divorce here, a troubled child there, too much fondness for dirty martinis or insider trading or some skirting of what everyone could agree were obscenely large tax obligations. Residents dined in Manhattan's best restaurants, sailed the Long Island Sound, which lay to their east, and spent weekends in repose in their stately turn-of-the-century homes.

Mark's own yellow clapboard home, built in 1901 in the Arts and Crafts style, was three floors of arched wood molding and mullioned windows. Inside, colors like cardinal (used in the library) were chosen from decorators' selections.

Mark now lived among the CEOs, flush with stock options, and revered bond traders—there was even a trophy in a shop downtown to commemorate the world's most talented executives—executive editors of news magazines and those, as the local joke went, who had made expert choices of parents, zygotes with foresight who had inherited vast sums. Where the money came from was no issue. The neighbors—as well as Mark—were life's shoo-ins, all members in good standing in certain circles.

Wealthy by his own hand, well married, admired by those in the corporate world for his reasoned outlook, expediency, and mindful nature, and with "one heckuva challenge" ahead of him, as he termed this entrepreneurial endeavor under the umbrella of a multi-billion dollar multinational, Mark was at the zenith of his professional career.

In addition to Kreamer, Mark also needed a media-savvy lawyer to smile for the news cameras, one able to make snap judgments about how different legal tactics might play out in the public square. After his move East, Mark hired Michael "Mickey" Sherman, who was based in Stamford, Connecticut, an easy ride from Pelham. Born in nearby Greenwich, Sherman's clients were among the most privileged members of society. Sherman represented Michael Skakel, a cousin of Robert F. Kennedy, who was convicted in the murder of Martha Moxley, another cold case that involved someone being bludgeoned to death. (In this case, Moxley's skull had been crushed by a golf club in Belle Haven, a gated section of Greenwich.) He also represented Alex Kelly, a child of means from Darien, Connecticut, who fled on the eve of his double rape trial and spent nearly a decade living the high life in Europe at various ski resorts. Sherman helped negotiate his surrender from Switzerland and even testified at Kelly's subsequent trial that he had advised the eighteen-year-old Kelly, just before he took flight, that there was no way he would get a fair shake in Connecticut.

Although Sherman's legal instincts in media-genic, high-profile cases (tabloids noted during the Skakel case that Sherman even resembled a Kennedy) were sound, on the odd occasion, they were questionable enough to elicit puzzled reactions. For instance, while representing a man charged with shooting ducks from his Long Island Sound yacht, Sherman ostentatiously walked into the courtroom with a pair of fake duck feet protruding from his brief case. Overall, Sherman was a clever lawyer—imperfect but clever—and, in terms of standing in society, a suitable match for Mark.

Kristina had moved from the Frito-Lay division of Pepsi back to Pepsi proper, which was based in Westchester County, right near Pelham. Now she served as head of marketing for Pepsi's diet beverage division. Pelham was wealthier than most of its neighbors, but assiduously low-key in a way that befitted Mark and Kristina's standing as well compensated yet private citizens.

Parmalat was located in North Jersey, which was better known for its Meadowlands swamps, but the commute from prestigious Westchester County was a small price to pay. Mark and Kristina's new three-story, $1.3 million dollar house sat on a choice block of understated elegance typical of the Sound Shore, as the area abutting the Long Island Sound was called. Their house had six bedrooms, five bathrooms, and seven fireplaces; the property taxes alone ran nearly $30,000 a year. The house was large enough for not only Mark's growing family, including their daughter, Charlotte (and, before long, a son named Eric), but also Mark's children from his first marriage—Julia, Emily, and Stephen, who would often visit. Susi had relocated back to Kansas after their divorce. Theirs hadn't been a contentious one, and Mark was generous, paying spousal support to Susi even after she remarried and started her own full-time career as a mental health therapist. He flew the children in once a month for weekend visits, and would even fly to Kansas to see school track meets. Ironically, his kids went to the same local high school as Paul Morrison's children. On the rare occasion when both were sitting in the grandstand, they kept their distance.

At pre-trial hearings—including a big one in May, 2004, at which Melinda's statement to Wall and James was challenged but ruled admissible—Mark's staff of five lawyers was omnipresent in the courtroom gallery, furiously typing on their laptops. Their presence in the modest-sized Kansas courtroom—especially the presence of the telegenic Sherman, who seemed to take up twice the space of any other lawyer on the team—projected an aura of unshakable confidence.

It was also in 2004 that one of Mark's Pelham neighbors, John Launer, a prosperous retired soap executive, began receiving a series of anonymous letters. Inside envelopes without return addresses, Launer found old Kansas newspaper clippings about poor David Harmon, bludgeoned beyond recognition. Scribbles from the sender in the margins of the articles told John in unmistakable terms that evil had arrived at his doorstep.

Launer discreetly brought the letters to Mark's attention.

"I have no idea who would send those," Mark said, allowing that he had been a suspect in the murder, but claiming that the then district attorney had given him a gentlemen's agreement, in writing, never to charge him.

This implied repudiation was more than enough for Launer, who, in his retirement, had become obsessed with Mark and the case. John knew Mark, one of the few fellow Democrats in a village that traditionally did not suffer them lightly, as an intrinsically decent, clear-thinking man. Mark seemed settled in Pelham, though he had moved around a bit, which was par for the course for those in search of the corporate prize: your CEO moment, as it was called locally. Mark was one of the few men John felt he'd trust with his own children and once, when he anonymously said as much to a reporter writing a story on the case for a national newspaper, Mark cannily figured out it was him and sent John a nice thank you note, which counted for a lot.

However, the anonymous letters continued. They had begun arriving just as Mark arrived to the neighborhood. The letters were sent to many of his well-heeled neighbors, who were naturally offended by the forwardness and unsubstantiated nature of the accusations—though some were half ashamed to find themselves a more than willing audience. They'd run across their wide lawns with the packages in hand, only opening them once they reached the privacy of their homes.

Their voyeuristic guilt was amplified as Mark—most came to conclude soon after meeting him—was simply an enviable man who had the fundamentals right. There was a fair amount of consensus about that. Even those who had hunched, thrilled, over the letters could extol Mark's virtues.

One day, after receiving yet another mysterious, anonymous letter, John Launer decided to pop the question.

He approached as Mark stood in his front yard, leaning on a rake. At a powerful 6'4", 220 pounds, and not a touch of gray in his hair, Mark seemed transported from his college days with only a slight bit of wear. It was his clean conscience, he had told an old acquaintance. As John regarded his neighbor, a cadre of high-end gardeners dressed in white descended on the vast lawns of the neighboring houses.

"Did you kill him?" John asked, at once disturbed to realize that his question came simultaneously with the sudden rev of lawn equipment. John looked at the gardeners. And again at the Harvard-educated Mark Mangelsdorf.

The gnarly accusations against Mark, no matter how injudiciously leveled, added a noticeable element to the mix of civil mindedness and old-money elegance that was more traditional local custom. Living in a bastion of such high net worth and low crime, it didn't happen every day that one of their numbers was accused of wholesale slaughter. The privileged were titillated. But this did not provoke direct confrontation.

That is, until now.

Smiling thinly, John laughed, but the laughter came out brittle. Almost like a sigh, though it probably passed unheard because of the noise of those machines, which was incessant. He excoriated himself for waiting so long to ask the question and finally doing it at precisely—to the split-second—the wrong moment. With few alternatives springing readily to mind, he tried again, nearly shouting above the gathering din:

"Did you do it? Did you kill him?"

Why the sudden notion that this had been the right opportunity to ask? John couldn't say, but not being absolutely sure of his instinct about Mark's innocence was threatening to lead John's entire worldview down a rabbit hole.

John, who could manage the large-scale sale of soap with the best of them, realized he was worn to a nub with worry by the roar of lawnmower engines and Weedwhackers and by the non-responsiveness of his younger neighbor. Was Mark leaning in close to hear what he may, in fact, not have heard? Or had he heard and was he, to John's utter disbelief and horror, actually trying to intimidate him?

When the subject of the case came up, Mark would try to make light of it. He would roll his eyes when he spoke of the curiosity seekers who drove by his house after his address had appeared in a local newspaper. He playfully acknowledged at one point that his circumstances, his story, in this setting, seemed lifted from an English mystery novel. A story, Mark added, he'd rather be reading than living. It was all like a game of Clue, right in their own parlors, a game based on equal parts of luck, skill, and intuition.

Thankfully, for Mark, there was no shortage of advocates like John, and who better to vouch for Mark than the neighbors, whom he had invited into his home for stollen, which he had baked himself, around the holidays?

And yet: was Mark really leaning in?

If John's ability to reason was reaching an apparent vanishing point, he could be forgiven. In spite of his reticent nature and all the social mores and niceties, John had, to his credit, finally asked the question that had long stalled so corrosively on his lips.

But how much, if any, had Mark heard?

In the quickly passing moments, John tried with all his powers of observation to gauge Mark's reaction. It was either thoughtful, angry, or nonplussed, which did not narrow it down. Would he have to work his way up to asking the whole question again?

John took a deep breath. He stifled an alarming impulse to belly laugh at the whole surreal exchange. He had cast himself in the role of amateur investigator; he had to forge on. He raised his sights up toward his neighbor to let loose one final stab at the words.

"Mark, did you murder him?" John now all but simpered.

It was all the fault of the letters, John thought, for putting him in this awkward position. He never should have dignified them with his attention.

Surely this man, replete with talent and conviction, could not have had a downward spiral at any point in life so steep that . . .? But even in the unlikely event that Mark had done the deed, we all had the capacity to do evil, so what set him so apart? Considering all the good he had done in life, the good children he raised, the jobs he created, perhaps there could be a time when culpability ended.

Why then, John asked himself, was he so thrown and frightened? He was sure of Mark's innocence, convinced of it.

John was informed enough in the field of psychology to know it was bunk to think of Mark as a sociopath. Even assuming he had done what the letter writer and now authorities were now sort-of, semi accusing him of, the behavior never repeated itself.

Had circumstances once aligned themselves in such a way that Mark had done the unthinkable? If so, that did not make him a sociopath—though how could he have gone on so apparently devoid of worries?

Proof positive that he had not done it.

John, glancing around at the busy lawn mowers, realized the noise would not abate. The air was filled with the scent of cut grass.

Mark leaned forward, furrowed his brow, and John saw a puzzled blink. Or maybe two. Mark had not been trying to intimidate him, in the least. He just hadn't heard him, which, in the end, John supposed, was for the better. Let questions about this ill-fated David Harmon linger. Like most on Loring Avenue and in Pelham at large, John already had a perfect sense of where things stood.

* * * *

After their marriage, Mark had become an occasional visitor of Kristina's grandmother's Presbyterian church, over in Scarsdale, an even tonier suburb than Pelham. Kristina's faith kept her firmly in Mark's camp, but in truth, Mark's religious beliefs had now become a part of the orderly managerialism that he used to run his life. Together, Mark and Kristina were winners of innumerable corporate competitions, which gave them social currency. They were among the most successful brand managers in the United States. You could talk to any of the people who knew Mark in a work setting, and every single one of them would claim that he was assiduous in his dealings, a firm believer in fair play, gentle in his treatment of subordinates, and remarkably advanced in managerial resourcefulness. He stood by business-school principles of order and forethought, and had a true gift for collaborative leadership.

That such a man had the capacity for such grave moral error was inconceivable. And even assuming Mark had committed one horrible act, did it matter at this point? The rest of his life appeared splendidly lived. He was a credit to his community and, in fact, every community in which he had ever lived.

Save, possibly, for one.

* * * *

With the heavy volume of anonymous hate mail accumulating in the mailboxes of Mark's friends, neighbors, and colleagues, especially as the legal case heated up after Melinda's indictment, Sherman hired Colluci Investigations, a detective agency in Stamford, Connecticut, to reveal the identity of this avenging angel. Perhaps the unmasked letter sender would be found to have had a role in the crime. Perhaps this was someone trying to deflect blame by putting pressure on false suspects like Mark. Whatever the case, Sherman wanted to pull the cloak of anonymity off the letter writer if only to get him or her to stop making Mark's life miserable.

Colluci used a handwriting expert from Westport, Peggy Kahn, who determined that all the notes and scribbles were written by the same person. In addition to the annotations in the margins of the old newspaper clippings about the case, there were notes—most handwritten, but some typed—on blank white paper. Key points were often underlined.

A note to one of Mark's neighbors in Pelham said:

> *Can't wait to tell the bank, your neighbors, friends—school— everyone needs to know, <u>he isn't what he says</u>.*

Another, written in the margins of a *Kansas City Star* article, this one about Melinda's indictment, read:

> *Mark Mangelsdorf has to pay for murder. David Harmon was a wonderful man and Mark <u>murdered</u> him. Mark <u>acts</u> real nice, doesn't he? But here is what he did. He <u>has</u> to pay.*

An obituary of Mark's mother was included. The sender had circled the lines reading, "She instilled [in her children] her belief in the innate goodness of others and an appreciation for the beauty of the surrounding world. She imparted to them seeds of the personal relationship she enjoyed with her Lord and Savior," and written, "*Really?*"

Letters were also sent to a host of neighbors in the historic district of Charleston, South Carolina, where Kristina's parents, Susan and Eric Friberg, lived.

Said one note:

> *Susan and Eric Friberg need the support of their neighbors and friends. The Mark Mangelsdorf in these articles is their son-in-law, married to their daughter Kristina. This is a very serious situation. Mark took part in taking another man's life, a terrible thing, and then went on living the good life as though it never happened, also a horrible thing. How can a person do that? Meanwhile, David Harmon has no life at all, and his parents have suffered every day of their life since. Mark needs to go to prison for this, and his family, including Susan and Eric, need to NOT protect him because to do so is to take part in the very evil he has wrought.*

The letters also came to Kristina's parents and Mark's father, directly addressing their support of Mark:

> *Why on earth would you want to support someone who took a life, and is unwilling to take the penalty for their awful deed? Why on earth?? You can love and support him while he is in jail, paying the price to society for murder—support him all you want*

then. But why on earth would you fight to keep him from paying for what he did? Because you choose to believe his lie? How self serving is that—on your part!

Colluci got a break when atop an old *Kansas City Star* article printed out from the newspaper's website were the words "Welcome Marian." Affixed to another article was an e-mail address that had started arriving in the inboxes of reporters, alerting them to new developments in the case. With the e-mail address, Colluci easily traced the mailings and letters to Marian Fuller, a secretary at a church in Manhattan, Kansas, who had been working in the same capacity at the College Church of the Nazarene at the time of the murder.

Even a defense lawyer could not claim Fuller as a potential suspect, but she had known and loved David, and was frustrated beyond description at how easily Mark had evaded criminal consequences. After Sherman's phalanx of investigators identified Fuller and wrote her a letter threatening legal action, the career church worker stopped sending the haunting packages but still managed to keep reporters abreast of the latest news.

Six

The threads of the accusations against Mark Mangelsdorf finally came together on April 4, 2005, in Pelham, New York. On this inordinately cold spring night, only a week before Melinda's trial was scheduled to begin, Mark was up late doing his taxes in the large, dark wood-paneled dining room. His home had more than doubled in value during the housing boom. The house could probably have been put on the market in the morning and sold by dinnertime.

It was around 10 P.M. when Mark's phone rang. John Hynes, a detective from the Village of Pelham Police Department, was on the line.

"Could you come outside, please?" asked Hynes, who had a direct way of conducting business. He was one of two detectives working out of a brick building headquarters, once the home of the Pell family that founded Pelham in 1654. Murder investigations were not exactly Detective Hynes's stock in trade. Hynes and his department primarily concerned themselves with the rather orderly work of chasing boozed-up teenagers. This was something new, and Hynes wanted to make sure Mark's arrest was done by the book.

Mark hung up. "I have to go," he told Kristina, who was pregnant with their second child.

He stacked some receipts into a pile, neatened a folder of bank statements, then went to the front door where, over twenty-three years after that fateful day in Kansas, he was put in handcuffs and formally arrested for the murder of David Harmon. There was no time for a good-bye to his wife, not even a farewell kiss. Kristina shook as she watched Mark unceremoniously taken away. She stood in their doorway as if shackled to the doorjamb.

* * * *

Mark was formally indicted on a breezy morning two days after his arrest, in the sleek Westchester County Criminal Court. It was no secret that Morrison's intention was to indict Mark in the early April lead-up to Melinda's trial. His status as an un-indicted co-conspirator would furrow the brows of the jury especially if, as expected, he was called as a witness. As Mark's lawyer, Mickey Sherman, put it at the time, "It's not like he was indicted because the FBI phoned to say they found a bloody print. It's not like they found a smoking gun in the past week or month." Without Mark's indictment, the theory that Mark and Melinda killed David to be together would sound half-baked, and Melinda would probably walk, which meant Mark wouldn't even be brought to trial.

At Mark's arraignment, he was brought into the courtroom with a group of other men from a holding cell. When one of the men's indictments for child molestation was read aloud, Kristina buried her hands in her head.

Once his turn finally came, Mark waived his right to challenge extradition to Kansas. His handcuffs were removed and he rubbed his wrists before signing the document allowing for extradition. A legal challenge would have only delayed the inevitable. Mark was then ushered out of the courtroom and later onto a plane sent specifically by the state of Kansas to take him back to Olathe. He was supposed to be flown to Kansas on Friday, April 8, where he could make bond then quickly return to the comfort of his home. Sherman wanted him back with his family for the weekend. When Kristina brought clothes to Mark at the Westchester County lock-up, she did not bring enough for an extended stay.

By the time Mark's plane landed and a van took its sweet time bringing Mark back to Olathe for the first time since May 1982, it was almost precisely 5 P.M., too late for his court hearing. Mark, wearing a green polo shirt and khakis, his hands shackled in front of him, had to be taken to the brown brick Johnson County jail to stew over the weekend.

After posting $300,000 bond on Monday, Mark left Olathe immediately, catching a commercial flight back to New York, leaving his team of lawyers behind to attend the jury selection for Melinda's trial.

* * * *

Jury selection began on Tuesday, April 12, and as spectators gathered for what seemed the dark reunion of everyone related to the case, one question loomed over the proceedings: Where was Dr. Wilmer Lambert?

John Harmon had seen Lambert only once since the terrible days surrounding David's funeral. He had always held Lambert accountable—for strong-arming the police, and for casting Sue and him out of the family the moment David was killed.

"If it were not for Lambert and the hierarchy of the church running interference," John would say years later, "David's murder would have been solved back when it happened."

In the years since, John had run into Superintendent Lambert at a regional Nazarene event, and the two had not spoken; but John had caught sight of Lambert and Lambert of John. John saw the wear in his face. Some bit of conscience, it consoled John to think, must be at play.

But how could a good Christian man take comfort in another man's psychic pain? John's soul was at stake here—bitter, lasting hatred was not a Nazarene option, and despite his suspicions, John remained devoted to his local church and a devout Nazarene. He knew he had to push himself toward forgiveness, or the crime would have another victim.

Lambert never showed up at Melinda's trial, but in his place Melinda's husband, Dr. Mark Raisch, maintained a daily vigil, never missing a court appearance. He was undeterred in his support for his wife despite the brutality of the crime, the ridicule the case brought on his children at school, or the fact that his thriving dental practice took a hit after the allegations broke. Also maintaining a daily vigil at the trial was John Harmon; however, his wife, Sue, could not be with him. A few days after Melinda was officially held over for trial, Sue passed away from her struggle with diabetes and heart trouble. The end had come suddenly. Sue had once dearly loved Melinda. Now Melinda was on trial for the murder of Sue's only child. John was convinced that the shock of Melinda's indictment, all these years later, was the final blow for Sue.

Joy Hempy, the queen of the Patron's Bank circle of women who had looked after David, was a fixture at the trial. This group of women had been gathering for lunch each year on the anniversary of David's death to remember him and reconnect with each other. Joy had not missed a single hearing date leading up to the trial, out of respect for David's memory and, partially, due to her obsessive interest in lurid murder cases. She was quite taken, in particular, with Mickey Sherman, a man she had seen countless times both on Court TV and as a commentator on the latest real-life murder drama to make its way into American living rooms. She would often send Sherman trivial emails, complimenting his tie, for example, and he would respond. It may have been Sherman who tipped Mark off that Hempy, as the most visible of David's non-family members in the courtroom, might also be the most vulnerable to his charms.

When Joy's nose was buried in a book during a break in one of the endless series of court hearings, she felt a gentle tap on her shoulder. She looked up to see a man all but blocking out the overhead lighting.

It was Mark. The man who had given much of Olathe nightmares for years was standing right there, all smiles, as if Hempy and he were old friends.

Mark introduced himself, extending his hand. It was a gesture, thought the bookish Hempy, pulled right out of Dale Carnegie's *How to Win Friends and Influence People*. It happened so quickly, though, that she could do nothing but play along.

"And this is Kristina," he said, pushing his pregnant wife forward.

"You look wonderful," was all Hempy could manage to say to Kristina. She was too polite and startled to say anything meaningful—or hateful—to Mark, a lapse she regretted.

Another daily fixture at the trail was Andy Hoffman, who had, in a series of annual columns in the *Olathe News* appearing on each anniversary of David's death, repeatedly called for the case to be reopened and solved. Now he was reporting as a correspondent for the *Columbus Dispatch*, Melinda's hometown newspaper, and noted that on the days he did not file a story, both Melinda and Dr. Raisch sought him out and thanked him profusely—on account, they said, of their children, who were eleven and fifteen at the time of their mother's trial.

Melinda's jury was composed of five women and nine men, including alternates, all of whom were white. This was somewhat of a mixed blessing. Whites on Kansas juries tended to be conservative, almost immovably inclined to convict. Then again, considering Melinda's original story, maybe it was best for the defense that no African Americans were called to serve.

To some of the locals packing Judge James Leben's courtroom for the three-week trial during the spring of 2005, Melinda's only redemptive quality was the fact that she had clearly suffered the ravages of time. Whether she lay in bed night after night tormented by guilt or was just genetically predisposed to aging badly seemed beside the point. She had left town a beautiful young woman and returned worn and bedraggled, confirming their notion that even those who evade the law cannot escape from the long arm of the Lord.

The two men hired to keep Melinda from ever facing overt punishment were Tom Bath, a hotshot lawyer, and Randy Austin, a handsome, elderly man who had been her original attorney. Brought in by her father in 1982, Austin had told District Attorney Moore after Lambert had his run-ins with police that Melinda would only answer questions if they were first submitted to him in writing. Austin was called back to the case these two decades later; though Bath, more active and current in the law, did nearly all the work.

A graduate of University of Kansas Law School, Bath had played a role in some of the most notable murder cases involving privileged suspects in eastern Kansas, including that of a beloved music professor charged with staging his lover's death as a suicide by wedging his neck into the base of a decorative wrought-iron bird cage. A typed suicide note was found later on the dead man's computer. Bath was also involved in the case of Thomas Murray, a linguistic expert who stabbed his wife to death in the neck a dozen times, also beating her in the head with a club, later telling police: "There's no such thing as the perfect murder . . . the bad guy always gets caught."

Murray, proper and urbane, sat at the defense table reading *In Other Words: A Language Lover's Guide to the Most Intriguing Words Around the World*, as the jury filed in to declare him guilty.

In the normal course of life in Olathe, people's paths often crossed several different ways, and Bath and District Attorney Paul Morrison, who were once colleagues, were now adversaries. Bath, like Morrison, had worked as an assistant district attorney in the Johnson County office. Both young lawyers had excellent conviction records and were held in high regard by their colleagues. Several years younger than Morrison, Bath was affable and slight, often standing at an angle with a hand on his hip, as if to keep his suit pants up. He liked the rough-hewn nature of state criminal court and had an uncompromising nature that served him well in court. By 1992, he had been named Prosecutor of the Year in the Johnson County office and wasted no time in leveraging the public service award into a lucrative private practice.

The Lambert family could afford the best possible representation for Melinda. They chose Bath because many of Bath's Johnson County murder cases came from the upper echelons of society, at least more so than the casework of most criminal lawyers in eastern Kansas. In that sense he was an easy pick for the Lambert family. His soft-spoken demeanor, his accommodating presentation—no one could genuflect for a judge as well—were a marked contrast to the tactics Melinda's father had employed in protecting her during the first go-around. Bath could sometimes lull the other side into a false sense of security. On bad days, his manner had been known to lull a juror or two into slumber.

Paul Morrison employed a different approach, both in life and in the courtroom. Tough and pugnacious when questioning witnesses (he was periodically admonished by judges for examining witnesses too harshly), Morrison was a gut player, a man with high moral aspirations. And while he did have his sights set on higher office, Morrison did not seem to be the typical duplicitous political player, but a Kansan with a loyalty both to the truth and common decency.

Melinda's trial came at a complicated point in time for Morrison. Long established as the district attorney of Johnson County, his political future was suddenly in flux.

Precisely as Morrison was preparing for Melinda's trial, his arch nemesis, Kansas attorney general and Republican Phill Kline, a crusader against abortion rights, went a step too far, even by Kansan standards, and subpoenaed the complete medical files of scores of women who had had late-term abortions. Kline claimed the measure was meant to root out crimes like statutory rape, but many, even those who considered the teachings of Darwin heresy, saw this as a ploy to embarrass and intimidate women who had had or were considering an abortion. To make matters worse, a Wichita abortion practitioner who'd contributed $150,000 to Chris Biggs, Kline's 2002 general-election opponent, saw his patient file particularly hard hit by the subpoenas.

Kline, once seen as an immovable force, was now viewed as vulnerable in the coming year's race for attorney general. Democrats in the state approached Morrison about switching parties in order to take Kline on with the backing of the Democratic Party.

Few thought Morrison would do it. A law-and-order Kansan was unlikely to drop the Republican affiliation that had served him so well. But in the end, he did just that. With this as the background, against the advice of every peer and political prognosticator in the state, Morrison brought murder charges against Melinda and Mark, two successful, wealthy, white Christian citizens in a highly circumstantial cold case and vowed to prosecute both himself.

Morrison had a sensible precedent for his actions. Employing the often risky strategy of trying big and particularly challenging cases personally, Morrison had lost only a small fraction of the cases he had tried as an assistant district attorney and had a perfect record as a district attorney. He won against Richard Grissom, Jr., convicted of three first-degree murders of young, beautiful women even though none of the victims' bodies could be found. He also won a high-profile conviction against John Robinson, Sr., a fifty-nine-year-old grandfather who posed as a magnanimous adoption broker but was in actuality a serial killer, one of the first to troll internet chat rooms to find his prey.

Yet a loss in the Harmon case would be an embarrassment, ranking among one of the biggest acts of political self-sabotage in state history. It would kill any possibility of a victory over Kline in the coming election. To Morrison, though, pursuing these convictions was a simple case of concluding unfinished business, fulfilling promises he made to himself when he'd first visited the Harmon crime scene over twenty-three years ago. Only one thing could validate the risk: a guilty verdict. And he would go to trial armed only with Melinda's two contradictory stories, the fact that she was the only one definitely at the scene of the crime, and a series of chaste love letters. There was still no murder weapon, no definitive confession, no DNA linking her directly to anything but the scene.

For a man with high aspirations, it was quite a gamble.

* * * *

During opening arguments, Morrison spun a yarn for the jury about how Melinda, a member of such prominent standing in the Nazarene church, saw widowhood as preferable to the condemnation she would face for divorcing David. "In her twisted world, it was better to be Widow Harmon than Divorcée Harmon," Morrison said. Bath countered that the Harmon marriage was strong, and that even if it hadn't been, divorce, if not encouraged, was tolerated—at least more so than murder—in the Nazarene community.

"Back then, all it took was a fifty-four dollar filing fee and a fifteen minute hearing," Bath said, scoffing at the prosecution's contention that divorce was problematic in any way, shape, or form.

Melinda watched the court proceedings slouched at the defense table, only whispering to her lawyers on the odd occasion. No lawyer in his right mind would put Melinda on the stand. Her conflicting descriptions of the crime scene implied guilt, and she would be easily susceptible to Morrison's technique of roping people in with soft questions, then hitting them with full-throated destruction when they tripped up. Mark, though, was considered by the defense to be an even match for Morrison, and had publicly stated his willingness to testify for either side.

Until Mark was called, the trial seemed to be biding its time. Neither the defense nor prosecution could draw up the perfect case.

It was not as if there were no evidence. There were, at least from an instinctive gut level, plenty of circumstances that did not quite add up for the defense. Melinda's dueling stories, for example—one as half-baked as the other. And the love letters. And Richard Bergstrand's account of having spied Mark and Melinda kissing. Melinda's blood-spattered pillow, too, didn't sit right when she claimed to have been sound asleep, presumably with her head resting atop it, as the attack began. Instead, Melinda had blood on the lower portion of her nightgown, as if it had been splattered as she had stood to watch some of the attack from a safe distance. That mattered little, though, in terms of imposing the burden of proof, especially at a time when jurors tended to demand exhaustive physical evidence.

The trial featured a hit parade of old witnesses. LaRue, grown heavy, had fled Olathe after retirement because he found it too bustling, and had taken refuge with survivalists out on the far side of Pomona Lake, due south of Olathe. He retold his story to the jury, testifying that Melinda had claimed she and David were in the careless habit of leaving the back sliding glass door open and that nothing was stolen from her home but the bank keys.

Gayle Bergstrand, still elegant and trim, told about that night and the sounds coming through the wall, and of how Melinda never seemed to lose her equilibrium. And never even asked after David, even with all those EMS workers attending to the scene.

There were new witnesses too—among them DNA experts who shrugged and said that the blood samples were not copious enough, not to mention too degraded, to determine a match with David's blood with more than 98 percent certainty. Absolute certainty—the benchmark for modern jurors conditioned by *CSI*—was absent.

On the same day that LaRue took the stand, a pair of doctors testified for the prosecution. Dr. Andrew Kaufman, a neurologist, and Dr. Richard Dubinsky, another neurologist who also taught at the University of Kansas, both stated that there was no way that Melinda could have been knocked out for an hour and then recount perfectly the events that led up to the strike.

"It does not happen," said Dubinsky, who was qualified by training and life experience, having once been hit by a car while riding his bicycle. It was almost like being hit by a pipe wrench. Dubinsky lost six hours of memory to an abyss.

Two days later, Gary Dirks, who was at the murder scene collecting samples for the Johnson County Crime Lab, confirmed that tests on the shower curtain in Melinda and David's bathroom indicated blood, more prevalent lower on the curtain he tested. This implied that the killers may have taken the time to clean themselves, though Sally Lane, who conducted the modern-day tests for Johnson County, was unable to make a precise DNA identification due to the age of the sample and the fact that it had been unfortunately stored at room temperature.

Dirks could not remember if there were towels or any other evidence of a cleanup, details that might shore up his theory.

The next day went along similarly. The apparent blood found on the rug inside Mark's apartment, which had been seized by the police in 1982, was determined then with 98 percent certainty to have come from David. Modern investigators could do no better. According to Shawn Weiss, who did advanced testing at a laboratory all the way in North Carolina at great cost to Johnson County, they weren't even certain if the DNA sample came from blood or sweat, which could bolster Mark's contention that David, heavy and overworked, must have innocently dropped sweat on his rug while helping him move.

Neither side had achieved any sort of terminal velocity. The verdict could go either way. Confident in the impression he'd make and how he would mount the final—and meticulously stated—effort to tilt the proceedings in Melinda's favor, the defense did what everyone had been waiting for all along. Roughly two weeks into the trial, the defense called Mark to the stand.

Over the course of Melinda's trial, dozens of witnesses testified as to the worth of the physical evidence, the possible state of her marriage, and the combative behavior of her father, but, for most trial watchers, Mark was the only witness that mattered.

Bath's aim was simply to poke at the prosecution's contention that something more than a friendship existed between Mark and Melinda. Mark was happy to oblige. If Mark came across as tame and reasonable instead of a dark spirit capable of gale force anger, the prosecution's story would automatically drop a notch in the jury's eyes. And speaking of the prosecution, another part of the subtext that day was whether Morrison's characteristic grilling of witnesses would lead to him lashing out at Mark in a public scolding. Which man with a catalogue of accomplishments might crack or stumble first—Mangelsdorf or Morrison?

An even bigger question that day was just how Mark and Melinda would react upon seeing each other. For all anyone knew, this was the first day they had been in each other's presence since a sobbing Melinda had leaned her head on Mark's shoulder at David's funeral, when he was seen whispering something inaudible, but widely speculated upon, into her ear. What would their reactions be?

In the moments before Mark's appearance, Kristina took a prominent seat along the aisle in the front row. Then Mark strode confidently in, his eyes on the witness stand to what seemed the exclusion of all else. At the front row, he bent down to give Kristina a short, almost perfunctory kiss. He then made his way to the stand where he was sworn in to tell the truth, the whole truth, and nothing but the truth.

Mark didn't look in Melinda's direction once during his testimony. A few moments after he settled into the witness box, Melinda whispered something to her lawyers but did just as admirable a job ignoring Mark completely. Whatever secrets these two former devout Nazarene Church members had to share with each other, they would not divulge them now, not even under an oath sworn before God.

After Mark had given the ages and names of his children, Bath asked him about his employment at Parmalat. Mark had been brought in as a senior vice president, with the charge of creating the international beverage giant's carbonated beverage division.

"Parmalat," said Mark, "is a global consumer product company that focuses principally on dairy products."

"Such as?" asked Bath.

"Such as milk. It's principally milk, shelf-stable milk, some fluid refrigerated milk. And then through Canada, it's a lot of cheeses, yogurts, other kinds of dairy products."

The testimony was interrupted by the blast of a train whistle. This was typical Olathe, the way conversations, transactions—really life itself—would come to a temporary halt because of whistle noise. It was an irony that whenever a Morrison trial was stopped cold, it just might be his brother Jack driving one of the 120 trains now coming through the town daily. Like their father and grandfather, Jack had become a railroad engineer, continuing a family tradition that from time to time gave Paul literal pause in his own job.

Bath then began a gentle round of questions about Mark's academic performance in college. Mark would be hard pressed to make an irreversible mistake with this line of questioning, which suited Bath's aims just fine. The more the jury liked Mark, the more they would think of the prosecution's theory as a lark.

Bath went on to question Mark about his meeting Melinda, letting Mark describe the platonic nature of their friendship. Mark also attempted to explain away the sometimes charged emotions displayed in Melinda's letters. For example, Mark said that one letter's reference to frustration at the guarded expression of feelings was in fact about his impatience over Melinda's refusal to dish on exactly how and why she got Dean Smith fired. Bath grazed over the topic of the other women Mark was dating at the time before trying to neutralize several of Morrison's anticipated lines of questioning, including why

Mark had moved off campus, to the opposite side of Olathe, just before the murder. Mark described it as a prudent financial decision; one in which David had played an advisory role.

After Mark recited a list of denials, including his having never kissed Melinda in any capacity other than as a friend, he made an empathic declaration. "Let me be very clear," he said. "I was not in love with Melinda Harmon." Mark hit the witness stand with the side of his balled fist. He probably intended it as a gesture of emphasis—it had a prepared quality to it—but perhaps he hit the wood harder than planned or mistimed the distance his hand had to drop. Several in the courtroom jumped.

"I did not have a romantic relationship with her, none of that," he said. "Melinda Harmon was my friend."

"And how about David Harmon?" Bath asked.

"David Harmon was also my friend," Mark said.

Bath wrapped up by leading Mark toward his favorite topic, the gentlemen's deal that district attorney Dennis Moore had offered him over two decades earlier. Mark had told everyone from his Pelham neighbors to Kristina about it. Moore wrote that if Mark came in with Hugh Kreamer, his lawyer and Moore's predecessor, and spoke honestly about the case, there would be no charges, and Moore would "consider the matter closed."

No one else was at that meeting, but Mark said that when asked point blank by Moore, he said he did not kill David.

"And did you kill David Harmon?" Bath asked.

"I did not kill David Harmon," Mark said.

Now it was Morrison's turn. In questioning witnesses, Morrison usually took one of two paths, depending on which might yield better results. The first was a casual approach, addressing a witness as if they had run into each other by chance and he hadn't given much prior thought to his line of inquiry. A witness did not have to make a grave error, however, for Morrison to dial his voice down to a guttural tone. That was the start of the second path, when his voice would begin to turn churlish, revealing a quick change artistry that owed more to his Irish ancestry than his Midwestern upbringing. He was never aggressively sarcastic, though—Morrison had too much Kansas in him for that.

For cross-examination, Morrison had several avenues of attack to choose from—Mark's platonic take on the letters, or the way he shat himself, for example—but he opened with Mark's oft-mentioned claim of a pseudo-deal. The only piece of paper evidence even tangentially related to the offering of a deal came from Moore in an October 13, 1983 letter to Scott Kreamer, in which he offered immunity for Mark if he took and passed a polygraph test. Kreamer wrote back the next day. "We are declining your offer," he said, because Mark had no confidence in lie-detector tests and therefore would not take one. Morrison and Mark went back and forth about what sort of offer was made and when, but neither gained headway.

Next, Morrison tackled Melinda's letters, asking Mark if when she spoke about deep, shared feelings that went beyond surface level, if that was the sort of chaste voicing one might use with a sister. Mark said it was.

"What does it mean when she says, 'I really don't ever want to suffocate you?' What does she mean by that?"

"Again, I'm not sure exactly," Mark said, in what was becoming a familiar refrain in regard to Melinda's letters. "I don't remember all of the details at the time, but I think she was just trying to be a good friend."

Morrison ran his tongue beneath his mustache and looked at him. "You have a lot of friends that suffocate you?"

"Pardon?"

"Have you had friends that suffocated you in the past?"

Mark managed a smile. "Probably occasionally, but not generally."

Morrison made some headway in cracking Mark's claim that the note about communication in his relationship with Melinda related to the Jim Smith firing. There was less traction when Morrison tried to frame his courtship of Kristina as an inappropriate office affair. Finally, he ended with a flourish concerning Mark's soiling himself on the night of the murder.

"We all know," Morrison said, letting his words drag out, "that diarrhea is a condition that when it hits you, you've got to go, don't you?"

"You probably need to, yes," Mark agreed.

Morrison brightened. "I mean, unless you're wearing a diaper when you got to go, you got to go, right?"

Mark agreed.

"And it can result in bad things happening to you and your clothing and all that stuff, right?"

Mark agreed again, before Morrison got Mark to also agree to the fact that he did not play floor hockey the day of the murder because of the diarrhea.

"And while you've got this diarrhea problem then, you decide that you are going to go on a big old walk?" Morrison asked, his voice now low and conspiratorial. He was referring to the walk Mark took with Melinda on the day of the murder while David was off playing floor hockey. The walk Mark had at first neglected to mention to detectives in 1982, a walk that was interrupted by a stopover at his apartment with Melinda.

"What," Morrison asked, his inflection mocking, "were you going to do? Were you just going to go behind a bush or something when you were out walking with her if you needed to?"

Mark said he never thought he'd be far from a restroom, but Morrison was setting a trap. "You would have probably been closer to a restroom if you would have been in a gym in a school playing hockey, wouldn't you?"

Mark allowed that this was a possibility and Morrison moved in for the kill. "In fact, when you went for that walk, Mr. Mangelsdorf, you stopped by your apartment with her, didn't you?"

"Yes, I did," Mark answered and Morrison promptly accused him of lying to police.

"I—I believe in reviewing the reports, that—"

"Yes or no, sir," Morrison demanded.

"—that's what I said on that day."

"What do you call somebody that doesn't tell the truth?" Morrison asked.

"I—I reviewed the—," Mark stammered, before Morrison cut him off.

"What's the word for that, Mr. Mangelsdorf?"

"I reviewed the events—"

"What's the word for somebody who doesn't tell the truth?"

"Forgetful."

"What else—what's another word? It starts with an 'L.'"

Mark shrugged meekly. "I don't know."

"Boy that's convenient, isn't it?" Morrison asked, not expecting an answer. He complimented Mark's memory in other aspects of life before ending his cross-examination.

Mark left the stand with the same confident, purposeful strides with which he walked into the courtroom. Later, Mark, Kristina, and his attorneys high-fived each other in the hallway outside the courtroom, apparently pleased with Mark's performance. Such enthusiasm seemed misplaced. At least the cross-examination hadn't led to a confession, though that thud heard as punctuation to his denial of loving Melinda seemed a poor move, a gesture eerily reminiscent of the crime of which he and Melinda were accused.

The jury foreman would later say that, like the rest of the jurors, he found Mark somewhat robotic and rehearsed. Outside of his errant reflex, Mark didn't let emotion divert him to the point of anger on the stand, but he was measured and modulated to a degree that seemed almost artificial. He aimed to elicit the perfect response, even if it meant not even uttering the word "liar" to the point of near absurdity. Yet there are far worse crimes than misplaced pride, and far worse fates than not appearing as perfect as the Divine.

* * * *

The verdict came down on a Monday, May 3, 2005, after little more than eleven hours of deliberation. There is an invisible crescendo before a big verdict is handed down. In that one moment, and often after long hours of dreary testimony, the courtroom almost exists in another dimension, a state of suspended animation where the only breaths taken are shallow and the only sounds heard are nervous twitter and the clearing of dried throats. Melinda's husband Mark Raisch sat tensely in the gallery, betraying no emotion. John Harmon looked drained, pale, and aged. Melinda, too, looked unmoved, not even betraying a sense of anticipation, though in a departure from her routine, she hadn't gone home for the weekend, either because she was confident she would be going home for good soon, or because she did not want to deal with the burden of a "final" good-bye to her children and home.

Melinda Raisch, the former Melinda Harmon, did not flinch when the jury declared her guilty of both first-degree murder and conspiracy to commit murder. Dabbing at her nose with a tissue, Melinda was immediately taken into custody. Her sentencing was scheduled for July 8, when she faced a stark fifteen-years-to-life sentence.

Mark, who had only flown in for his testimony, had already left Olathe when Sherman informed him of the verdict. Along with Mangelsdorf's team of attorneys, Sherman had been in attendance when the verdict was announced, taking notes.

"I don't believe it's doom and gloom on Mark's case," Mickey Sherman said in a statement outside the Olathe courthouse, a less than ringing endorsement of his client's predicament. "I think Mark will get a fair trial. This was the trial of Melinda Raisch. It's a different trial."

That Melinda was found guilty of conspiracy to commit murder did not bode well for Mark. Implicit in the verdict was the fact that at least this jury believed the prosecution's version of events, that Mark and Melinda had killed David in order to be together. Sherman could herald Mark's chances, but those chances had now narrowed considerably.

On the prosecution side, with Melinda convicted, the state's investigation was hardly in the end game. Quite to the contrary—it was, in some ways, only just beginning.

PART THREE

"For whoever keeps the whole law and yet stumbles at just one point is guilty of breaking all of it."

—James 2:10

SEVEN

Mark was facing trial—which would probably take place within a year—but the case against him was highly circumstantial. Morrison had the love letters, which would be dismissed by Mark's lawyers as typical of the flowery, friendly language between Nazarene friends. And in terms of DNA, the prosecution had evidence of human blood in Mark's vacuum cleaner (along with a neighbor's testimony that Mark ran the vacuum cleaner the night of the murder), but because of the degraded nature of the sample, they could not tell whether it was David's. David's DNA was found on the carpet in Mark's apartment just inside the front door, but again because of the age of the sample, they could tell with only a 98 percent certainty that it was David's. Coupled with the still-missing murder weapon and a fingerprint on the back patio door that Mark could have left at any time, the evidence left ample room for a jury to have reasonable doubt.

Morrison knew you could never predict what would happen in front of a jury. The case just might fly, but he knew, too, that *The State of Kansas v. Mark Mangelsdorf*, awaited for years in these parts, might very well drift sideways into acquittal. That would leave Melinda spending the rest of her life in prison for a crime she conspired to commit with Mark without Mark paying the price himself. Morrison knew he needed Melinda's testimony in order to convict Mark.

He began a rolling conversation with Melinda and her lawyers, trying to come to an agreement that would nullify her jury verdict—giving her the chance to plead guilty to a lesser charge and get a sentence reduction—in exchange for her testimony. The conversations made Morrison angry, though. Melinda seemed unwilling to admit total guilt. She kept pulling up close, then backing off, almost admitting to the crime, then disavowing her culpability—just as she did when Wall arrived at her doorstep that day in Ohio.

Morrison intimated that he might just take the risk of allowing Mark to skip scot-free, back to his life as a corporate leader and moral steward. Melinda and her defense team also got the idea, though no one is quite certain precisely how, that Wall and James had a good lead on the crowbar. Fred Jones, Mark's brother's friend who had acted as his lawyer back in 1982 (and was now an FBI agent), told Wall that he had once seen a receipt of Mark's for a crowbar purchased a week before the murder at a local hardware store. The hardware store was long gone, though, and the receipt was nowhere to be found.

Prosecutors obtained a subpoena allowing them to listen to Melinda's phone calls to her family from Johnson County jail in the hope that she would reveal something about the location of the crowbar. As soon as she plugged in her prisoner code for her collect call home, the bug would kick in. Then James, doing what he joked was "combat duty," was faced with the task of sitting on his back porch in the evenings with a big glass of wine, listening to the tapes of the recorded calls between Melinda and Mark Raisch.

The investigators wanted to know if Melinda knew more about the case than she claimed, but that's not quite what they got. The conversations between Melinda and her husband were awkward to listen in on—two Bible-thumpers making pillow talk and discussing the tedious workaday details of the lives of their children. Melinda was often self-pitying about her fate, and Raisch would answer back with reference to God's grace or God's plan to open doors, Bible passages, or offers to send religious magazines.

"Be faithful and the doors will open," Raisch told Melinda in a typical conversation. "I truly believe it, I truly believe it."

"How will the doors open?" Melinda asked.

"That's where God comes in," said Raisch.

During another conversation, the two spoke about their legal plans. Melinda bemoaned her fate, remarking that she was destined to rot in jail, while Raisch, who was in closer touch with her lawyers and seemed more aware that their conversations might be recorded, referred obliquely to potential future legal maneuvers.

"We didn't get the results we wanted," Melinda said, referring to her trial.

"There are ways around that," Raisch said assuredly.

"I hope," she answered.

"Appeals," he said. "The lawyer says we have a fair to good chance."

"But he said that about the trial," Melinda said.

"Can I send you *Guidepost and Angels*?" Raisch answered, not addressing her complaint but falling back on that age-old support that had seen Raisch through many a tough situation but had failed to offer Melinda much comfort as of late—faith. When Melinda beseeched Raisch at one point whether they would "make it," Raisch answered "When I am with you, my faith grows."

There seemed to be nothing of value to the prosecution to be learned from the phone calls. But then, in one call, James heard Melinda refer to a letter that she had written in which she said she had made reference to a crowbar. She was fretting about what to do with the letter and was worried that if she mailed it, it would be intercepted. The prosecutors immediately secured another subpoena, this one to search Melinda's cell at the Johnson County jail, where she was being held until sentencing.

Melinda was cleaning up some of the other women's cafeteria trays in her pod (she now headed up Bible study in the jail) when Wall and James arrived, but she still took time to greet both detectives as warmly as she had back in Ohio. Yet she surrendered nothing voluntarily, going back to her kitchen duty while they turned over her cell.

Wall and James were bemused to see that she had the same calendar that was in her home, with all her children's schedules written down, like a professional dispatcher. (On the phone, she would remind her husband of which errands to run, down to telling him where he could get the best price/value ratio for a birthday gift for one of the children's friends.) At last they emerged with a letter that was as rambling and self-pitying as the woman herself.

From his surveillance of Melinda's phone calls, James was familiar with her thought and speech patterns. Seeing more of the same—this time in print—made James yearn, even in the middle of a jail pod, for a big glass of the red wine that helped him get through the tapes on his back deck. He was buoyed, though, by the prospect of finding the reference to the crowbar he had heard about on the taped phone call.

Melinda's jailhouse letter, addressed to her husband, began on a note of despair. A visit by her lawyer had brought news that Paul Morrison's latest offer for her testimony was firm and final at twelve to twenty years, which would mean Melinda would have to serve about a decade before making parole. If she took the deal, she'd lose the right to appeal. If she refused the deal, she'd be looking at fifteen to life and, in what she felt was a cruel twist, "they will probably drop the charges on Mark M. They don't want him bad enough, I guess."

She was outraged that, merely because she "participated in this, and took part in the planning and then lied subsequently" about it, that she would be considered an "equal party" to her husband's murder.

Feeling pushed toward a plea, and wary of risking an appeal, she acknowledged in the letter that she knew Mark purchased a weapon a week before he killed David, but she gave no idea of where it might have been stashed. Short of what James was really hoping for—a treasure map leading the investigators to what they guessed would be a rusty, dirt-encrusted crowbar hidden somewhere just beneath the surface of surrounding Olathe—this was all he needed. Morrison could use the admission to put pressure on Melinda to make a deal or to turn up the heat at Mark's trial.

Melinda expressed a willingness to "do the right thing and help them get a conviction on Mark," but she also yearned for some kind of divine intervention on her behalf. "What do you think God is trying to say?" she asked her husband in the letter. "Some of God's promises are looking quite thin at the moment. I know the ones about the future are in place, though they're the ones about the Gate opening for us, and the waters parting, and Him being the Mediator that I'm struggling with." In a form of rough justice, Melinda was perhaps finally learning that redemption and salvation weren't necessarily the same thing.

Morrison had Melinda right where he wanted her, in a state of fear with limited options and unlimited time to turn them over in her mind. Mark's trial probably would not start until the spring of 2006, and he did not have to act until then. This time, Melinda was not going anywhere.

* * * *

Mark unexpectedly waived his right to an evidentiary hearing in late 2005. An evidentiary hearing would have given Mark's side the opportunity to grab a front-and-center look at all the evidence prosecutors would present against them, but they already had had a preview from Melinda's trial.

The reason for his decision was probably another unanticipated turn of events: Melinda had been invited by prosecutors to testify at the hearing against Mark even after being found guilty at her trial. She would presumably testify to yet another version of events (Mark definitely killed David) and, whatever details this would set in stone for eventual comparison at trial, the hearing would give her practice at telling her latest story in a public setting. Though practice might not make perfect in Melinda's case (word from Kansas was that she was giving Morrison fits, continuing to perform verbal contortions so as not to define herself as a murderess), it still might prove harder for Sherman to unsettle her at trial—as he was fairly certain he could—if she got in a practice round. Also, Mark's defense team didn't want potential jurors to hear any more from Melinda than was necessary.

The prospect of Melinda's testimony, though flawed (Sherman was already labeling her various stories A, B, and C to keep them straight), was worrisome to Mark's side. An even larger concern was Morrison offering Melinda an unconventional deal to get her to turn against Mark. Melinda had already been convicted by a jury, so giving her a deal at this point would be sidestepping—or nullifying—the jury's verdict. Her sentencing had been delayed several times, amplifying speculation. Would the jury verdict be stamped out completely, setting Melinda free with nothing more than time served? That would be quite the stroke of luck for Melinda, though probably not feasible. Such a deal would be a dangerous move for Morrison. At the very least, however, he would have to offer her a serious reduction in time to get her to admit guilt and testify against Mark in open court.

At this point, Mark was no longer with Parmalat. By coincidence, Parmalat had imploded just as the case against him grew more serious and more public. Bad luck, too, was Mark's presence at the company when it was revealed that Parmalat had falsified earnings and understated debt for well over a decade, earning the company the unwanted reputation as the Enron of Europe.

Parmalat's plan of starting a grand new business expansion, considering its self-inflicted circumstances and sad legal state, was relegated to the ash heap, and Mark was let go. With Parmalat insolvent, its leaders sought refuge in bankruptcy court. Senior officials were investigated, but Mark was excused from the proceedings because he hadn't been at the company long enough to be involved.

Mark had never in his business career been accused of improprieties. Morrison had been certain he would uncover figurative bodies lying in Mark's wake, as well as the one real corpse, but he could never find any. Neither could anyone else.

Under a murder-one indictment, Mark was not quite board-room material for the moment. Now he worked out of his home as a consultant, but defending himself—defining the Mangelsdorf brand—had become Mark's full-time job.

In yet another surprise twist, Mickey Sherman called this author, in my capacity as a reporter for the *New York Times*, to offer me an exclusive interview with Mark.

"Just you and him and Kristina, if she's available," Sherman said. "I won't be there, nor will any of his other attorneys."

It was quite an offer. I had covered the case for more than a year for the *New York Times* and, while Sherman trusted the fairness and accuracy of my previous articles, Mark had not sat for a single interview. The risks—especially without his staff of lawyers hanging over his every word—were obviously too great. Now, though, circumstances had shifted and Sherman was nothing if not a risk taker.

I called Mark and left a message. A calm and undemanding voice called me back in a matter of minutes.

"Nice to meet you, if only over the phone," he said. "Would you like to come over?" He said he wanted time enough to put his daughter to bed, so if I could arrive at his house after 8 P.M., it would be ideal.

We made small talk and Mark seemed accommodating and businesslike, his voice inclined more toward gentleness than your average high-powered executive.

Though Westchester County is a bastion of wealth, Pelham is less ostentatious than neighboring Scarsdale or Chappaqua, where the Clintons settled after the White House and students drive far more expensive cars to school than do their teachers. Not that the children were left without decent cars in Pelham. Here, though, everyone was a touch less conspicuous about it—a two-year-old Volvo might suffice instead of a new sports car.

A turn through a pair of old limestone gates that marked his neighborhood's boundaries led to Mark's street and house, both of which could serve as backdrop to any magazine feature on established wealth. No house was a duplicate of another, though most were broad, three-story structures. There were only a handful of front porches, and lawns were large enough to dissuade neighborly drop-ins, but the homes were classic specimens of the early 1900s.

Approaching Mark's house along the walkway, I saw that neither the grounds (the lawn was still unseasonably green) nor the front of the house were decorated for Halloween. Nothing trite or kitschy was on display or taped to the glass front door. A low curving wall of hedge protected the house itself. The yellow clapboard stretched up more than thirty feet to the roof, where two chimneys stood. A walk around back led to the covered slate veranda. Considering the mild nature of the night, I could have been heading to a garden party.

The front door was located behind a glass entryway, a pre-foyer designed to keep unseasonable weather out. I was about to knock lightly instead of pressing the doorbell so as not to wake their daughter when I spotted through the glass two figures at a service island in the kitchen. It was Mark and Kristina readying for my arrival. Mark was leaning in close to Kristina, apparently explaining something. His forefinger was thrust out aggressively toward her, and either the act of leaning down, or the force with which he was speaking, had drawn blood to his face. His lips looked drawn and tense. It was all pantomime and could have been completely innocuous in nature, but the silent tableau was an unnerving one to happen upon. There is always disquiet, a voyeuristic guilt, in stumbling upon the tensions of others, and while Kristina did not appear to be in any danger, witnessing that muted caliber of intensity was perhaps more frightening to me than if I had been able to hear the exchange.

I rapped lightly on the door and they both turned, their eyes widening, with welcoming smiles instantly on their faces.

They came and opened the door. Mark's voice was soft, seemingly detached from his brutishly large body. It was not a matched set. His build allowed for attack mode, but his voice made every effort to mitigate. They invited me in through the foyer and back to the kitchen.

I noticed a kids' playroom next to the kitchen, filled with neatly placed, candy-colored toys.

We exchanged pleasantries about our neighborhoods and a restaurant in my village that Mark and Kristina frequented. They asked whether I wanted a drink—wine or soda? Though I could have used the wine, or something stronger, I did not want to risk missing anything and asked for a Coke.

The Mangelsdorfs erupted in laughter. They opened their refrigerator, loaded with Pepsi products. I apologized for the faux pas (they laughed again) and sheepishly asked for the Pepsi I should have requested in the first place.

Sitting at their kitchen table, we started talking about their early lives and how they had met. Mark and Kristina were careful to parse out exactly when they had started dating, drawing a clear distinction between the time of Mark's separation and when they became involved. Their deft, poised statements already had the polish of a specific, pre-planned agenda, but that was to be expected. The two were well seasoned brand managers, and their brand—Mark's life—was hitting a crucial moment in its history.

Mark dryly allowed that, to be certain, he always expected this case would come back into his life. Given his experience back in Kansas, he said there was no reason to think it could not happen again. "Kafka come to life. Now twice," he said. Despite outward appearances all these years, apprehension had always been hovering.

Mark was not submitting to his fate, though. Being removed from the legal limbo of an unindicted co-conspirator gave him an unaccustomed sense of relief. The trial was a new challenge he actually seemed to welcome. "It's a little bit," Mark said, "like 'Okay, now the game is on.' I'm no longer wondering or anticipating if something is going to happen. Now the real show begins."

We discussed the collapse of Parmalat.

"I never saw it coming," Mark said about the turn in his professional life. "I really thought I had landed in a good place."

I decided to ask him, without any warning, if he had killed David, if he had indeed bludgeoned his friend to death while he slept. As questions go, it was an impertinent one, ill-suited for such a discriminating setting.

Mark looked straight ahead and, without sputtering or offering anything but his rigidly even eye contact, answered in his soft but unwavering voice, "I did not."

He did not take the occasion to elaborate. Kristina looked at him, and I looked at her, but Mark looked out ahead, first at me directly and then, for a good long while, at the wall of windows behind me, staring out into the night.

"Do you think about David a lot?" I asked, trying to come at the subject sideways and, at this point, to break the silence.

"Of course I do," he said, with a small trace of annoyance. "Not every day, but David Harmon was my friend. I miss him." It was curious to hear him use David's first and last name, and to hear his admission of thinking of David only on occasion.

When asked where the long and deep string of suspicions came from, Mark said the entire idea of him being the murderer was preposterous, but once a thought gets into a small town's mind, it is hard to dislodge. He was a suspect of convenience for the bumblers that passed for investigators, and now Melinda, who he had never known to be slanted toward lunacy or lies, was telling tales to save her own skin.

Making a plea agreement was not even an option open for discussion, Mark said, as Kristina nodded rapidly in agreement, though in criminal cases and in the minds of all practical, deal-making men, no overture is ever rejected for consideration before it is set forth. Considering the convoluted nature of the case, there was no telling what would happen. A good offer could chip away at a person's resistance, no matter how strongly stated.

When asked who killed David if he didn't, Mark raised his hands to the air and said he hadn't the foggiest idea.

"I only answered a call when a friend needed help," he said.

Mark was a matter-of-fact man, and this—all of this—was another run-of-the-mill situation for him. Kristina was less accustomed to such disorienting turns to life and was living in what she kept describing as a state of suspended animation. When Kristina visited Mark in jail during his week behind bars, it was with the seeping sense that they were living other people's lives. She said that the guards asked her how she ended up involved with someone she'd have to visit in jail. Kristina had managed a laugh, replying it was too long a story for words.

For Mark, the rhythm and pitch of jail was challenging, but he had no overwhelming qualms about his brief experience. He knew some of those he was jailed with were innocent and became friendly with those he would not consider "bosom buddies over the long haul," but who showed him the ropes during his short stay behind bars. "My husband the chameleon," Kristina suddenly laughed. "He'd fit in anywhere."

It was an un-artful and imprudent comment. A chameleon has some obviously pejorative connotations. Mark shot his wife a look, bristling ever so slightly as he leaned toward her. He managed to pull himself back, but his attention never wavered after that. The conversation resumed on an easier plane, and Kristina didn't say anything else that caused him to become visibly uncomfortable.

At the end of our interview, there was one last issue to iron out. The *Times* required a photograph to accompany the piece and in such circumstances, with Kristina obviously pregnant, the picture could not help but be compelling. I did not, as I often did, arrive with the photographer. I wanted to establish a rapport first and didn't want to scare off Mark and Kristina by the presence of an additional person with a lens and heavy flash. Talk to someone, and he can sometimes lose himself, forgetting that he is talking for posterity. Flash a light in his face while he talks, and he won't forget it's on the record.

Mark was all too eager to be photographed, especially alongside Kristina, who likewise very much wanted to be in the photograph but was concerned with how she would look. It was the end of a long day, and though she had not a hair out of place and looked beautiful, if a bit austere, she was feeling drained, lacking her usual level of physical confidence.

Kristina soon agreed, and I excused myself to call Susan Farley, the photographer, who was waiting by her phone at her home about twenty minutes away. She arrived in less than that, and Mark and Kristina were soon posing around their house, Kristina pushing out her belly slightly, perhaps for a more sympathetic-looking portrait. We kept the conversation going during the photo shoot, and Mark said, when asked, that he did not think Melinda had hurt David and that he, Mark, would never have been friends with someone who was off-kilter. She had either changed or was desperate to get out of jail, he said, referring to her apparent testimony against him, but that was a matter for Melinda, the courts, and her God.

The next day Mark emailed me a thank you note, along with a photo of him with his adorable daughter, Charlotte, who had slept soundly, in the same house as her father, through the night.

Eight

Mark Mangelsdorf was never a man to accept defeat, and it seemed—especially for anyone who had lent him an ear on the subject over the last two decades—unthinkable that he would ever admit guilt. There was nothing to admit to, he'd say. Mention the prospect of a plea, and Mark would respond as if it were absurd.

To a certain degree, Mark, like many in America seeking a better life, was always between skins. By nature Mark was, as his wife unwisely let slip, something of a chameleon. He only *appeared* steadfast and consistent. Whether Mark dropped religion to fit in better with the corporate establishment, or because he blamed the constricting hold it had on him for that one detonation of emotion, Mark shed a skin he was born in and—as a committed evangelical—reborn into. He went from being devout to, from all practical measures of church attendance, essentially becoming an atheist. He later shed the Midwest, and his college sweetheart, the mother of his first three children. He even shed any trace of his blue-collar existence, leaving every last remnant along the banks of the Mississippi. It did not seem likely that he would ever shed his claims of innocence, which had defined him for so long.

Yet circumstances had come to a serious point for a serious man. Morrison finally obtained Melinda's agreement to testify against Mark at his trial. In exchange, her jury conviction would be vacated, allowing her to plead guilty to a lesser crime: murder two, or intentional second-degree murder. She could then be sentenced to ten to twenty years in prison, and would be eligible for parole in five years. Kansas had no death penalty in place at the time of David's murder, but a conviction for first-degree murder meant the potential for life in prison. And Johnson County juries, culled from the area's conservative religious population, were not known for their leniency. Mark's life, at least as a free man, was in imminent peril.

By instinct and training, Mark compulsively weighed risk against reward. Like any good graduate of Harvard Business School who went on to hone his business skills at the highest level, this was part of what made him so good in businesses as diverse as carbonated beverages and uniforms, and part of what allowed him to excel in both operational management and sales. It was time for Mark to weigh his options and decide which would work to his best advantage. Nothing, not even a plea deal, was off the table.

It helped that Mark's lawyer had a gift for making trials go away with pleas. This skill probably surpassed Sherman's gift at trial. Sherman was always astute in how he presented his case before it even went to trial, prattling on to the cameras and note takers, coloring the perceptions of the jury pool or, perhaps, just striking fear into the prosecution that he had an airtight case and was willing to let a jury decide. When it came to negotiating a plea, Sherman had an uncanny reputation for patience and stick-to-it-ness. When a Stamford, Connecticut, client was faced with forty years for beating a teenager into a vegetative state, Sherman negotiated a plea for four years of jail time, and then argued for even less time at the sentencing. When he was castigated after the court appearance by a reporter who asked how he had the audacity to act in such a fashion, Sherman didn't respond with fancy word play or righteous indignation.

"It's the only way," he said bluntly.

Morrison, no slouch in weighing options to his advantage, had his own concerns. He had won cases with flimsier evidence, but this case he could just as easily lose—one that everyone was watching. Difficult, too, from Morrison's perspective, Mark's trial was scheduled for the spring, right at the start of campaign season for the fall election. Trying the case would lose him precious time on the campaign trail, time that a Republican now masquerading as a Democrat could not afford to lose. He had already won a significant victory against Melinda, and an acquittal for Mark would nullify that victory in the eyes of voters. If he lost, he would be chastised for tormenting Olathe all over again. At best, it would color him as a loser just as greater Kansas was getting to know him, a bit like a marathoner getting shot by the starting pistol. There were even rumors that Morrison would not try the case himself. Something—or rather, someone—would have to give.

It began to appear that both sides could benefit from a plea agreement. Morrison's first offer to Mark amounted to close to twenty years in prison for admitting guilt; this was a non-starter on Mark's side. In that scenario, Mark would be an old man by the time he got out. That was unworkable.

On Friday, February 10, 2006, Morrison called with an offer that even Sherman considered a good deal. Mark would plead guilty to second-degree murder in exchange for a sentence of ten to twenty years. Mark would have to admit guilt in open court and, obviously, give up his right to appeal. The intriguing aspect was that, with sentencing guidelines in place at the time, Mark could be eligible for parole in five years. This was a one-time offer, and Sherman would have to answer by Monday or it was off the table permanently.

A restless Mark immediately discussed the matter with Sherman in his Stamford office. Kristina came with him. By now, their second child had been born, a son named Eric.

"What do you think?" Mark asked Sherman.

"It is your time," answered Sherman. "It has to be your decision."

Mark and Kristina drove home in a light snow to decide. The storm escalated into a Nor'easter, dumping more than two feet of snow on the New York City suburbs, all but transforming them into what one could imagine a pastoral version of Chili looked like. John Harmon, who was now back in Chili with a fiancée, Regina Lappe, a preacher's widow he'd known through the church and who had come to his side after Sue died, would not be informed of the plea deal until he returned to Kansas, about to sit for what he thought would be another round of pre-trial hearings.

For Kristina, it was surreal to be left with such an insufferably difficult decision to make, so little time to make it, and, in the end, no hard facts—only their gut instincts—on which to base their decision. After all this time, and all the efforts of their legal staff hammering away on the minutiae of the case, they were left to make a life-altering decision with a simple "yes" or "no."

Mark, for his part, was better at clinical observation, and the deal looked pretty good to him. He knew Kristina could wait a few years for him—five years was a modest term—to get out, but she couldn't be expected to wait a space of time that stretched out well into old age.

Kristina always defined Mark by his ability to be considerate to others. She loved to tell the story to friends about how when she was pregnant with their first child, they narrowed their name choice down to either Charlotte or Catherine. Mark wanted Catherine, while Kristina preferred Charlotte. Kristina, who said she always found Mark to be the more giving of the two in their relationship, decided to give Mark the choice. He said they should wait until they saw what the baby looked like, though Kristina naturally assumed Mark would choose Catherine.

When the baby was born, Kristina muttered, "So what does she look like?"

"Charlotte," Mark responded. He then handed Kristina a Tiffany's gold locket. Engraved on the back was "I love you, Mommy! Charlotte." Mark had ordered it weeks before.

Kristina told Mark she needed him with her, eventually. Together, the two MBA graduates did a cost-benefit analysis of their own circumstances—the risk of trial versus the reward of Morrison's offer. She told him to take the deal. The issue, for her, was practical. To Kristina, Mark was a man undone by circumstance, nothing more. Or less.

Mark was told to fly to Kansas on Sunday so that he could be in court on Monday morning. For the first time since September 11, though, all New York area airports were closed on account of the storm. On Monday, Mark flew from New York, along with Kristina, back to Kansas, back to settle matters for good.

Dean Stelting, now an administrator at a different college in the Nazarene Bible school chain, when asked, angrily defended Mark's innocence even in light of the plea. But one of his sons, Damon, said he felt crazy for believing Mark, defending him to friends and co-workers in the immediate wake of the plea. Soon, though, he got a seeping sense of doubt, triggered by a nagging memory from back when Mark was staying with them as a teenage boy, of a single flash of anger.

Damon had mowed the Stelting's modest lawn, as he used to before Mark took up residence there. Mark had been handling chores like that more recently as thanks for their letting him stay. While driving Damon to baseball practice, Mark turned and snapped, "Why did you do that? That's my job!"

Michael Copeland, the current Mayor of Olathe, called Mark "as gentle and nice a man as I'd ever known." He had succeeded Mark as student body president of MNC.

Mayor Copeland said that it was inconceivable that his once dear friend, whom he had "totally idolized," could be involved in anything lacking in grace, much less infused with evil. As a student at MNC, Mayor Copeland confessed that he would drive with friends an hour outside Olathe to crack open beer cans, to get around the campus ban on drinking, but Mark—known as "strong and never wrong"— steadfastly refused. It was clear to all: there was no need to chase the devil from Mark.

In the hectic nights that followed David's murder, Copeland volunteered to drive home with Mark from nighttime student government meetings because the police tailing him were less apt to pull Mark over and harass him with a witness in the car.

Copeland was elected to the office of mayor in 2001. He said that on one of his first nights in office, he was riding in a police cruiser and leaned over to the front seat to ask the patrolmen if they knew anything about the David Harmon murder.

After Melinda's arrest, however, the questions came in the other direction when the *Olathe News* quoted Mayor Copeland saying that he was not surprised at the turn in events. This elicited a prompt call from Detective Wall, who delved into the exact meaning of his quote. Was the mayor actually implying, Wall asked, that he knew something? Mayor Copeland said that his quote had been taken out of context.

For Kristina, there was no question of Mark's innocence. "A leopard does not change its spots," she said. David Penrose, the psychologist for the criminally insane, who grew up and attended college with Mark in the same puritanical environment, also used a predatory animal metaphor.

"You let the lion out of the cage and then you try to get it back in," he said. Which is, of course, part of the story's end. Mark managed to put the lion back. And keep him locked up. This was not a crime committed at a distance, but close-up, one that sent a man's eyeball flying across the room. And while it was partially a crime of passion, he had planned it for months, lying in wait with a crowbar in his possession for a full week. But the lion was, forever afterward, caged and gentle.

* * * *

Mark wore a dark suit, a starched white shirt, and a funereal black striped tie to his February 13 guilty plea, nearly twenty-three years to the day after David was murdered. The fashion choice was quite a departure from the more traditional corporate red power tie he sported when he testified for the defense the previous spring at Melinda's trial and had refused, even when pressed, to utter the word "liar."

Morrison rose to speak, to give a public account of the murder and all of the suspicious behavior by Mark and Melinda leading up to it. Mark sat attentive at the defense table as all the years of conjecture, myth, and wild guessing were about to finally give way to an airing of the truth. Kristina was once again sitting in the front row, as she had during Mark's testimony, their children back in storm-hit New York with a babysitter. She cried throughout the proceedings.

Though he was pleading guilty and thus no longer asking for vindication, Mark was still angling for the deal most advantageous to him. Sherman argued that while Mark was agreeing to plead guilty to the crime, he was not signing off on every aspect of Melinda's version of events. By agreeing in principle to Melinda's statement of events, while not making a formal statement himself, Mark was effectively carving himself some wiggle room by implying that there were alternative explanations, or that he just might be getting forced into the plea by circumstance. And Mark, to be certain, offered no alternative explanation of David's murder. His caveat merely raised doubts, however subtly, about Melinda's story without correcting a single item of it.

Morrison rose to read Melinda's statement in open court. Between that and all the testimony and remembrances of those involved, the veil of the past could finally be pulled back.

Mark and Melinda became friends through contact at the dean's office. Mark was a man headed places, but inexperienced with women. Melinda was desirable and flirtatious, experienced but looking for someone new. A friendship blossomed and quickly deepened. By sometime in 1981, there were stolen kisses and perhaps there was nothing more salacious than that. Melinda introduced Mark to David and they became friends. When the couple went away and Mark stayed in their house to house-sit, he would count the condoms and admonish Melinda when some had been used.

Whatever the strange alchemy between them, Melinda was happier when Mark was around. God's love was strong, but this was stronger. For Mark, the headiness of this attention from an older woman, a fellow churchgoer—but one of such high stature and carnal knowledge—was all but unmanageable. He broke up with his girlfriend, with whom he had never even tried to have sex. Then he broke his lease and rented a place across town to be closer to Melinda.

Mark began to lament to Melinda that they had not met before she was married. Divorce was heresy, but on a lark Mark began talking about how nice it would be if Melinda was not married. He soon brought up the prospect of unhitching the brakes on David's car.

He decided against that idea, and weighed the relative strengths and weaknesses of other options, considering the situation tactically. Then, after Revival Week, he told Melinda that he had purchased a crowbar and "the time was coming."

Aware of Mark's plans, Melinda compared widowhood to divorce. She landed far enough on the side of widowhood to not warn David what was afoot. And to leave the sliding glass door unlocked. And to rise from the bed on the night of February 28, 1982, as a shadowy figure in a homemade cloth mask entered her bedroom. Melinda watched from a distance as the attack started before running downstairs to the living room.

Mark stood on the far side of the bed, nearest the bedroom door. David was lying on the side of the bed closest to the wall, which meant Mark was looking down at David's face as he brought the crowbar down with all the force he could muster. His arms were fully extended for the most destructive leverage.

There is no telling which of the dozen or so blows killed David. A precise count was unknown because of the nature of the injuries. There were no neat bullet holes or knife wounds to tally. Did the first strike of the crowbar kill David instantly? That could very well be—there were no defensive wounds of any kind. Or it could have been one of the next twelve blows to David's head, none of which were delivered sparingly. Rather than hesitating at any point, Mark was apparently invigorated, a soul wholly consumed.

One blow carried over to the next. When he missed David's shattered skull, his blows struck and crushed David's neck. The bones in David's nose and cheeks were pulverized, caving in his now formless face toward the pillow. One of David's eyeballs was ripped from its socket, landing on the light brown wall-to-wall carpeting. Blood and brain matter sprayed everywhere—against the white wall behind the bed, the drab brown curtains beside it, onto the dried flowers in the glass jar with marbles sitting on the night table, and into one of the night table's open drawers. The painted wicker light shade that hung from the ceiling was sopping wet with blood, as was the flowered quilt and the flowered yellow bed sheets, including the area where Melinda claimed she had been sleeping when the attack began. A rush of blood and brain had even splattered behind Mark, landing in the hallway that led to the bedroom.

When he was done, Mark went downstairs to find Melinda. The bottom hem of her nightgown was blood spattered from the few moments she spent watching Mark swinging the crowbar at her husband's skull. She asked Mark if he was sure David was dead. Mark went back to David's bedside with the crowbar and struck him again, pummeling a now lifeless body.

Returning to the living room, Mark and Melinda staged the mock robbery, taking the top to the key dish jar and placing it on the floor. Then Mark, as per the plan, lightly struck Melinda, barely enough to bruise her. She then, before going to the neighbor's for help, waited the agreed upon period of time to give Mark enough opportunity to clean up. Melinda covered David up, tucking him in with a final act of perverse tenderness, then ran next door to the Bergstrands, reciting the prepared story about the black assailants, the version that somehow held sway for over twenty years.

A final, macabre note—at David's funeral, when Mark whispered into Melinda's ear, virtually the entire town (including the police) wondered what he had said to her. Mark calmly told Melinda that he had gotten rid of the crowbar.

* * * *

Mark pled guilty to a charge of second-degree murder with a few attentive "Yes, sirs," to the judge. Under normal circumstances, an admitted murderer would be remanded to custody and taken out a side door to the Johnson County Jail, where he would await sentencing, then assignment in the state jail system. With Mickey Sherman on his side, though, Mark was given ninety days after his plea to get his affairs in order, a highly unusual arrangement, but one for which Sherman, in all his negotiating glory, had pushed. Mark walked out of the courthouse, squinting in the white light of the day's late winter sun, his gaze even more piercing, though when he spoke to the mob of cameras and notepads, he sounded nonplussed.

He explained the decision to change his plea, to reverse years of claims of his innocence, in the calculating words of a business transaction. "We considered it recently," he said. "It was time for me to plead guilty. Thought it was the best way to move forward and get things behind us."

Kristina still held Mark out as the perfect soul he had strived to be. "He's the best husband and father he could be," she said.

"I'm interested in serving the time as soon as possible so that my family and I can get on with the rest of our lives," said Mark to the trailing cameras and notepads.

John Harmon, in just an afterthought that day, told those same cameras and notepads—anyone who would listen, really—that he felt a measure of relief, but mostly sadness. Mark, he said, was speaking of his penance like an "appointment." John had prayed for Mark over the year, but with a mindset like that, how would moral regeneration ever occur, with or without the power of prayer?

There are always letdowns after long waits, but this was different. John's base instinct that the deal offered to Mark was a blessing had suddenly given way to an emerging reality. He was learning yet again that nothing would bring David back.

Nine

Desert winds from the west were running loose in Olathe, spiraling in different directions in the courthouse square. In its center stood a gazebo, where a cluster of lunch-time workers took refuge from a scorching Kansas sun. With his softly trembling hands clutching a packet of papers, John Harmon, who had always prayed for guidance on how to be incorruptible in his faith despite all that had happened over the years, ambled toward the front doors of the courthouse. It was May 12, 2006. The sudden end of David Harmon had come more than twenty-four years ago in a duplex just a few minutes' drive away.

Mark and Melinda were due to be sentenced for David's murder. The sentencings would unfold in staggered fashion, and John, never known for saying much except to his elementary school students, would be allowed to say whatever he wished. A man who always deferred to the preferences of others would get his final say. He had already started in the windswept courtyard, handing out protest fliers, some of which were immediately carried off by the arid wind. They had a pair of photos of David on them, one from when he was about twelve, the other from his early twenties. David was wearing a nearly identical sport jacket, white collared shirt, and tie in each—the shirt starched in the later photo, the smile a bit more ready in the first.

IN MEMORY OF DAVID HARMON, a caption on the flyer read. JUSTICE FOR DAVID, WE WANT JUSTICE, and JUSTICE OBSTRUCTED, JUSTICE DELAYED, JUSTICE DENIED! ran across the top in large bluish-purple Magic Marker letters.

John's fiancée Regina was beside him. She was a different woman from Sue. Regina actively pushed him along in his new role of avenging father, capable of handing out flyers demanding justice, something that for the old John Harmon, with his entrenched concept of Christian forgiveness, would have been unthinkable.

When sentencing came up at Melinda's trial the year before, John had told Paul Morrison that she should be spared jail time altogether.

"You sure?" Morrison had asked, apprehensive. He pushed John along toward a tougher stance, knowing that John's religious ideals would give way to human nature. Morrison had been right, it turns out—and he hadn't needed to push John too far.

When Morrison told John that Mark had agreed to plead guilty and would agree to serve a term of ten to twenty years, John was elated and signed on immediately in utter disbelief. He didn't understand, of course, that parole could be in as little as five years. Now John, perhaps with Regina's help, felt he had been duped into accepting the sweetheart plea deal expected to be ratified today.

Morrison, now smack in the middle of a race for attorney general, defended himself, saying he had explained the deal thoroughly, and was reacting to the realities of a tough case that, at the very least, would put both defendants behind bars for at least five and a half years. Mark was aware that, while this would be a short enough time for Kristina, it might not be short enough for his father, who was living in Wyoming in declining health. Ray Sr. had not made any of the court appearances and, barring a miracle, would not be able to visit Mark in jail when the time came.

During the three months between Mark's plea and his sentencing, he took the opportunity to visit his father (now widowed and Catholic) in Cody a final time, a layover appended to a long vacation he'd taken out West with Kristina, all five of his children, and his brother Ray.

Inside the courtroom, where Mark was to be sentenced first, the familiar faces began to gather. The Jakabosky brothers swapped old floor-hockey stories with a former MNC student, all of whom had a good laugh about Mark's official title his junior year in college being "sergeant-at-arms." Joy Hempy, David's friend from Patron's Bank, was there as well.

She had recently played a starring role as herself on *48 Hours,* a documentary television show that covered the Harmon murder case in an episode. Hempy was filmed walking down the aisle in an Olathe supermarket, throwing groceries into a grocery cart, pretending to shop as she spoke about the case. A production assistant ran behind her, retrieving each crashing grocery item (which with luck did not ruin the sound) and restocking the shelves. The bank ladies who watched the show when it aired guffawed when Mark and Kristina were shown, playing themselves, on a couch together reading the Bible, going so far as to point to certain passages.

In the aftermath of David's death, the bank ladies had taken food offerings to his widow, even as they kept an eye out for the attackers who might yet try to gain entrance to the bank. They knew then how politically charged David's wholesale slaughter would become; who knew then who and what Melinda Harmon really was?

After handing out protest flyers in the courtroom hall, John, followed by Regina, took his seat across the aisle from Kristina and her parents, who sat behind the defense table. When the call came to order, Mickey Sherman was nowhere to be found. He was in the bathroom, the court was told, and Kristina laughed with resignation, rolling her eyes at her parents. There was more general chatter among the benches of the courtroom, and discussion of the "after party," to be held at the Bergstrands'. The Bergstrands had moved, and everyone who had seen their well-appointed new home was talking about it to those who hadn't yet.

Mickey came running in moments later, giving Joy a small wave. There was a second call to order, but such was the reputation of Judge Thomas Bornholdt that there would be no need for a third.

John Harmon was given his choice of whom to address first: the court or Mark. John saved the more charged confrontation for last. Perhaps he had to work himself up to it.

"All right," John said to Judge Bornholdt. "I guess I will start with you."

John went on a long, pre-planned tirade on the terms of the plea, how Morrison—so focused on his political future—had all but fast-talked and tricked him into it on the February day they had gathered for Mark's pre-trial hearing. At the ensuing guilty plea, John said, the sound system was so bad that he could not hear all the details.

John said he had been the victim of a gag order since 1982. His voice was rising.

Morrison's bald head turned red and he let it fall into his hands. Plea deals often left victim's families somewhat short of satisfied. They were a necessary evil, but this was a delicate matter, especially during a political campaign. Morrison would have to do damage control when he made his statements, but this was John's turn to speak after twenty-four years of silence. He thanked the judge, before asking if he could turn and speak to Mark.

"Can you hear me, Mark?" said John, the waver in his voice more obvious as it rose. This was not a volume at which he ever spoke—except on the rare occasion he wanted to quiet a boisterous schoolroom.

"Yes," Mark answered, sitting thick-shouldered and stiff at the defense table.

"Mark, I met you once before when David introduced you to my wife and myself. I waited for twenty-four years, twenty-four years to talk to you in just this setting. My comments to you, Mark, are based on what I have observed, heard about, and read about your life since that fateful day in February, 1982. I'm just drawing conclusions based on your actions and your behavior. Actions have consequences. Mark, when Melinda and you conspired to commit premeditated murder, you both unleashed a chain reaction of consequences that continue to this very day. And I guess I'm very much afraid will continue to the future that will affect you and Melinda and your respective families."

Kristina, sitting with her parents behind Mark, had been poised and self-composed, but here she dissolved into tears.

John, who believed so much in Jesus as a champion of peace, was warning Mark and Melinda—however obliquely—about God's potential wrath. But he was not jubilant about it. John went right from all that Mark would one day have, to what he, himself, never would. "Your senseless act took away any chance we had for grandchildren. Mark, in some ways I do envy you. You have five children. Chances are that at some point you'll be blessed with grandchildren. Do you have any idea, any remote concept of what it feels like when well-meaning friends talk about"—at that John paused and caught his breath—"and show pictures of their grandchildren in my presence? It tears me up every day inside." John then summed up Mark's fairy-tale life before struggling one last time to find meaning in the action that had nearly rotted his soul.

"In spite of all you have done I forgive you unconditionally, but I am filled with sadness for you, Mark," he said. "[With] the chain of reactions that you started, you've destroyed yourself. What a waste. What a complete waste of human life. I also still pray for you now—maybe, just maybe, Mark, deep down inside your psyche, someplace, somewhere there still lingers a tiny bit of conscience. Maybe, just maybe, that will get and bring you to a complete and honest reconciliation with your God. Then, once that is done, you can start on the road to restitution. I pray, Mark, I truly pray that God has mercy on your soul."

Detective James then testified, speaking about how, when he, Wall, and Paul Morrison took up the case, it was still an open wound to the community and the Olathe Police Department. He did not reach for higher meaning. "What penalty could provide comfort for the family of a murder victim?" James asked rhetorically. "I don't have an answer for that. What I do know is that David was described as a kind and gentle man by those who truly cared about him. And I know he most certainly did not deserve the sentence he was given."

Then without any pause or ceremony, it was Mark's turn to rise.

"Thank you, your honor," he said. "I'm Mark Mangelsdorf and I would like to make brief comments, if I may. And if it's okay, I would like to turn around so I can address Mr. Harmon."

"You may," said Judge Bornholdt.

"Mr. Harmon, I can't even begin to imagine the grief and sorrow you and your wife experienced for the loss of David. I can tell you as a father of five how much I love my children, and I know the special bond that exists between a parent and a child. So what I can say is that I'm truly, truly sorry for David's death and for the loss of the time that you've experienced not being able to spend time with him. There has not been a lot of time on a lot of days since 1982 that I haven't wished I could turn back the clock and do something that would change the events of that night. I thought of David on that horrible night and I wished that I could change something to bring him back but I can't, of course. What I do know is that I have pled guilty to this. I've acknowledged my involvement and I hope in some small way that helps for you to have some closure to this. While I can't go back, and I wish I could, I can't."

Mark went on to say that he had tried to live an admirable life since David's death and his effort was genuine. "So," Mark continued, "my commitment going forward is that I will in every fashion that I'm able to continue to try to do what is right the best I can. And for the foreseeable future, I don't know how that will play out, but I will look for those opportunities, however that exists. I am sorry. I'm very sorry."

And with that stutter step toward contrition, Mark thanked his wife and in-laws for standing by him as if he was accepting the grown-up version of the Pioneer Award.

The judge told Mark to rise and sentenced him to the anticipated ten to twenty years. Kristina finally lost her reserve completely while Mark was being cuffed and led away. Scott Kreamer, acting quickly, arranged with a guard for Kristina to spend a moment with her husband in a room behind the courtroom.

* * * *

Mark's sentencing was, with few exceptions, a premonition of Melinda's, which took place two hours later in a courtroom upstairs. It was the same crowd, in a tighter space. Melinda sat pale, slight, reduced, her hair no longer highlighted, wearing the striped Johnson County Jail jump suit. The matter of John's opposition to parole commenced the proceedings. "I just want to be sure that the defendant does understand before we proceed with sentencing," began Judge Leben, a slight and professorial figure who seemed perched upon the bench, "that Mr. Harmon's position is that this has no guarantee from him that he will not oppose her receiving parole at any particular date, and that with that understanding, she isn't asking to withdraw her plea."

She wasn't. Who would be? Months ago, she was facing life. Now, with one year to her credit, there was a good chance she would be out in four short years. She would take her chances against John Harmon's wrath, perhaps winning him over for the second time in her life. Paul Morrison then preemptively defended the plea agreement yet again. He pointed to the savagery of the murder, noting how difficult the case against Mark would have been without Melinda's assistance. Punishing Melinda for life with Mark free as air would have been one final note of unfairness in what had already been a long convoy. To defend the plea deal, Morrison essentially had to defend the inherent decency of Melinda, a convicted murderer.

"I can assure you," Morrison said, looking down at his papers, without the verve he used at trial or on the campaign trail, "that Mark Mangelsdorf would not have pled guilty to second-degree murder were it not for the fact that Melinda Raisch had agreed to help us. Now, did she do it as an altruistic act to help humanity? I think not. I sincerely doubt that. I am sure she did it to secure a lesser sentence for herself. But as the Court is well aware, sometimes that is necessary in a criminal justice system to make it work as well as it does, as imperfect as it is."

Morrison defended his dealings with John, revealing that at one point he had to ask John to remain silent about his wish that Melinda be given no jail time so that they could work toward a compromise. He said the only reason John's name was not on the plea agreement was that John was in Chili when it was typed. John, for his part, gave Melinda the same speech he gave to Mark when it came time for him to speak, the same cadences, the same points-of-emphasis, substituting the name Melinda for Mark, but in substance leaving it at that, save for one crucial departure.

"Melinda," John said, "I hold you more responsible than Mark. You, as the wife, could have called a halt to the plot at any time. You could have stopped it." In his rage, John had come a long way from telling Morrison that he wanted Melinda to skirt jail altogether.

Then, another departure. Regina asked for an opportunity to speak to the gallery. Her statement came out in a torrent. It was long and, to the increasing discomfort of those in attendance, dense. The technicality that she did not know David did not slow her down. Morrison, forehead in his palm, was staring down at the state's table. But John gazed up at her, rapt.

"Do we really know if Melinda did or did not commit other criminal offenses before she murdered David or since she murdered David? The records would tell if we were aware of them. Well, one thing I can rest and have assurance in is God knows. He holds all our records. Thank you for being allowed to speak my heart to this courtroom on behalf of the silence of David Harmon. Sincerely, Regina."

It seemed the end was at hand. "Your honor," she said, "may I speak to Melinda?"

There was an uncomfortable fidgeting in the courtroom. Judge Leben seemed to blanch. "Yes, ma'am," he said, before adding, "is it brief?"

"Not really," she answered, scoring, at the least, a point for honesty with the fidgeters.

Judge Leben told her she had to be. As the attention in the courtroom continued to unspool and a bit of sympathy even crept Melinda's way, Regina spoke about the comparative stigma of divorce versus murder and the need for Melinda to get a psychological evaluation, with a final demand that Melinda pay restitution in the form of an amount equal to the $40,000 in life insurance that she collected. "With interest," she said.

Finally, mercifully, Regina was done. Melinda was given the opportunity to step up to the podium to speak. When she got there, though, she pivoted to speak to the assembled instead of the judge, squinting in the light and cupping a hand to her eyes to help her see.

"John, where are you, I can't see." Embarrassed, she laughed, too flippantly for the occasion.

Melinda had acquired an unhealthy pallor during her time in the penitentiary. Her eyes roved about the first two rows in the hopes of settling on John.

She caught sight of John and laughed casually again. "Oh, there you are." She then turned toward the judge.

"First of all, Judge," she began, "I wish to express my deep remorse and sorrow for ever having been involved in this. I am extremely remorseful and horrified that this event ever occurred." She spoke in the passive voice, a common tactic—both strategically and subconsciously—for those who want to put distance between themselves and an action. Mark had used it as well. "I in no way intend to minimize it," she then said. "If I need to be specific about my guilt to you today," she said, "it is that I had knowledge about this event occurring and that I lied about it subsequently. It is a shame and remorse that I will carry with me the rest of my life."

"To the Harmon family, I am really," she stammered, "I am really sorry. Words do not adequately express the things I feel in my heart. Just words are not enough. I would love to have better than words. I just don't. I am very, very remorseful and would in no way ever expect any amount of time to make up for this.

"The life of David Harmon was an inspiration to all who knew him, including me, and I am horrified beyond words that I was ever connected to this."

John Harmon shifted in his seat.

"I knew the minute it happened that it was wrong, and I was scared to death and didn't know how to be strong enough to tell the truth about it. For that I am very, very sorry. I also apologize that I have not had the chance to contact Mr. Harmon all these years. I would have done so but was prevented from doing so by my attorneys, and through my year of incarceration here I have also been prevented from contacting him in any manner. So today is the first chance I have had. I am very, very remorseful. David Harmon was an uplifting and very caring person to all who knew him. They would agree with that. I considered him to be a fine example of how to live a life. I greatly missed him from the moment of his death, and I will always miss him for as long as I live."

Tom Bath, Melinda's defense attorney, then rose to speak, immediately conjuring up the judgment day—the one with the upper-case J—that Melinda was still due to face. As both a prosecutor and defense lawyer, the low-key Bath had learned that such references tended to fare well in Kansas courtrooms.

"She understands that she has got to serve a sentence that is determined by man, and there is a sentence that is going to be determined by a higher authority," he said, beseeching the judge to consider Melinda's help in bringing Mark to justice. He added by way of explanation that Melinda did want to meet with John in private, not to sway him, but simply to avoid doing it in public. Melinda also wanted to pay back the life insurance funds she collected from David's death even though they were not a formal portion of the restitution required by the court, and negotiations were ongoing. In short, Melinda had done everything possible to end all of this cold-blooded business, and Bath asked one last time that the court honor the plea struck by both sides.

Before adhering to the deal, Judge Leben made one last futile stab at making sense of it all. "Since moving to Ohio, and especially in the period following her marriage to Dr. Raisch, the defendant has led an exemplary life," he said. "The Court surely cannot know and I do not know her motives. I can't make a finding about her motives. Perhaps she has been trying to make amends for her past crime. Perhaps she has simply regained her senses and truly possesses a strong moral character as so many of her friends attest and David Harmon once believed."

The judge shrugged. He then officially sentenced Melinda to the ten to twenty years proscribed by the plea agreement. Perhaps it was because she had already been jailed for a year, or because there was relief that she was serving much less than the possible life sentence she faced, or because the overflow crowd had lost their way in the torrent of words, but there were no tears for Melinda as she was taken away.

* * * *

What John had always wanted had now come to pass. The culprits had been brought to justice, but it simply wasn't enough. Even as Mark and Melinda were carted off to serve out their sentences, he was neither consoled, nor lifted, nor cured by any stretch of the imagination. He and Regina filed outside to the foyer and then the courtyard to hand out more protest flyers. Many were taken and John was given pats, platitudes, furrowed brows, and serious nods. Other flyers were lost in those hectic winds, which blew that whole day long.

John was left without the feeling that justice had been served, and without any persuasive answers as to why his only son had been murdered. While Mark had longed for acceptance, John had finally been brave enough to risk losing it. And look at what it had earned him—a half-hearted apology from Mark, a repeated passel of apologies from Melinda, and a sense that he had disappointed those who had done the most to bring this case to some form of conclusion. Though he knew what had happened to David and, on a superficial level, why it had happened, the question of how two people who had the capacity to live such otherwise decent lives were capable of such brutality remained unanswered. You can solve a mystery, John realized, without having answered any of the questions it posed.

And look at how the two who guarded the answers could change their natures and be rewarded. Even Olathe, changed irreparably in its nature, could rest in self-satisfaction now that the most unsightly blot on its recent history had been set right.

John lingered in the hallway outside the courtroom, then walked downstairs and out into the beating sun of the courtyard. "We're protesting the hand slaps given to the killers of David Harmon," John intoned, time and again, trying to sell his story. News cameras trailed him and those with notepads and fast angling pens did too, but to no effect, other than to earn him the occasional sympathetic nod.

And at that, the story of David Harmon, from the public's perspective, was over.

Ten

Until her sentencing, Melinda had been held at the Johnson County Jail in Olathe. Two weeks later, she was transferred to the Topeka Correctional Facility, the state's only all-women's prison. Considering her age, otherwise unblemished record, and potential release date, which stood less than four years from her arrival, Melinda was assigned minimum security status.

The bright light of official prison photos gives a high degree of scrutiny to facial features and skin, but Melinda looked almost unreasonably happy. Her shoulder length hair was well-kept, but no longer streaked with blonde, and her face was nearly aglow with a friendly smile. Given her almost childish laugh and behavior at her sentencing, it seemed Melinda would consider it bad form to show anything but a pleasing façade to the world.

Melinda was living in a dormitory-style setting with mostly non-violent drug offenders many years younger than her who looked to her for motherly advice. She was still as self-obsessed and self-pitying as always, forever in search of the loophole that would get her home before her anticipated parole date of April 29, 2010, but she was doing what little she could to better her small corner of the world. She led a Bible study class, and used her full weekly allotment of phone time speaking to the girls in the dental office, her children, and her husband, who visited her regularly. She seemed lifted up by an unseen force, and if she had doubted that force was God immediately after her conviction, there could be no doubt now that she was a true believer, someone whose spirit has been left fully intact. God would one day fairly soon allow her to return to Ohio, where she hoped to pick up where she left off, though with her children five years older, much will have changed.

As for Morrison, he rode the press attention that surrounded him after the trial straight to the office of Kansas Attorney General. The press took even greater notice when, on his way home from his new office in Topeka in his pick-up truck, Morrison saw a Doberman pincher attacking an old woman's little dog and, screeching to a halt, dove on the bigger dog, allowing the woman to pull her pet to safety. He did not call a press conference, but the news leaked when the woman called the media herself. It was political theater of the most favorable kind imaginable. Here was a man who had managed to switch to the Democratic Party and still trounce a Republican in a state President Bush had carried with well over 60 percent of the vote. Now he was saving old ladies' dogs and not even using his gallantry for political gain.

The whispers about "Governor" Paul Morrison grew louder.

And then, a year into his term, Morrison was accused of having an affair with a married woman named Linda Carter, in his old office, where the defeated attorney general, Phill Kline, had been appointed to fill Morrison's old post. Morrison was even accused of spying on his arch-nemesis Kline through Carter, digging for information about the controversial abortion case that was still on-going. And, as if any other tawdry details were needed, he was also accused of demanding Carter get a tattoo that matched his. Carter sued for sexual harassment and Morrison, who with his wife taught marriage counseling at their Catholic Church, denied all her accusations except for the affair. Nevertheless, he left office and political life in disgrace only weeks after the accusations surfaced.

"I have held others accountable for their actions, and now I must be held accountable for my mistakes," said Morrison in his resignation, just as a criminal investigation was getting underway. Kansas had not seen a fall from grace as dramatic and swift, it was noted darkly in state political circles, since Mark Mangelsdorf woke one morning in a multi-million dollar home and went to bed in a prison cell that night.

Morrison's bad luck was self-inflicted, but Wall and James saw luck run the other way because of forces out of their control. The two had the best cold-case heads to display on the figurative mantle in Olathe, and their future posts seemed sure to reflect that. The Olathe Police Department, however, soon became fixated on an automatic rotation in posts, and Wall and James lost out. James was moved to internal affairs, the departmental equivalent of eternal damnation. Wall got put in charge of giving lie detector tests, which was as ignoble an appointment as James's because most of the tests were given not to suspects but to potential hires, to see what secrets lay in their past.

Those who knew Wall as a man who could sell a false bill of goods as well as anyone—a detective who had tricked suspects with lines of total nonsense—could only laugh at the irony of him now being set loose in search of verbal inconsistencies in others. If you asked, Wall would say he was always in the business of inconsistent stories.

"It takes a bullshitter to know a bullshitter," Wall said with a crafty smile. "But a machine helps." For a detective who operated on little more than a hunch, a lie detector was a little too scientific a tool for comfort, and the only knocking on doors in Wall's foreseeable future would come from those potential employees arriving at Wall's office to be grilled by a machine.

Both James and Wall hoped that in their future there would be one more door for them to knock on—the one to Mark's prison cell. They wanted, more than anything, to hear an unqualified admission of guilt, a complete account of the killing from Mark's own mouth, in Mark's own words. They wanted an accounting of the thought processes that led a pious young man to believe murder was an acceptable solution in the eyes of God. They wanted, too, to hear an apology that rose to the level of the act he had committed. The fact that he had not gone far enough in his admission in court could still turn the two sour. They planned to ambush Mark with a prison visit, telling him they would haunt him at all of his future parole hearings unless he came totally clean. Over two years after the sentencing, they still hadn't gotten around to that yet, busy as they were with their new assignments.

* * * *

The first photo of Mark in prison, taken during his formal processing, showed a frightened man. Against the backdrop of a cinder-block wall, in an unforgiving bath of whitish light, Mark's shoulders were rolled slightly forward, giving him the look of a man reduced in size, his courage failing. His eyes were wide, even bulging, as though he was trying to ward off whatever bad was coming. There was no bravado, no armature, no posturing.

Mark, for a change, was in harm's way. And he knew it.

After languishing in the county lock-up for two weeks after his sentencing, Mark was first taken to Kansas' most modern prison, El Dorado, in an area of Kansas along the Walnut River known only for refining oil and interning prisoners. In addition to housing the state's most notorious inmates—like Dennis Rader, a church president, civic advocate, and convicted serial killer—El Dorado is where all inmates are taken to be classified. At the Reception and Diagnosis Unit, a battery of psychological and medical tests, as well as the cataloguing of professional histories, is performed. Mark was held in solitary confinement during the diagnosis process in a cell more stifling by the day in the emerging heat. He joked on the phone to friends that he felt "like a Tandori chicken."

Despite the heavy air and loneliness, Mark's period of solitary confinement held its advantages. At least he was on his own and safe. As prison adversaries go, sexual predators were not Mark's first potential enemy. At his size, Mark had the look of a man who could fend for himself, not one who was young and vulnerable. Of greater concern were the extortionists, those who knew from news accounts that he was a man of means and could lean on him to have his family make their canteen accounts flush—or else. Then there were those with whom one came into contact on a daily basis who, with match-strike tempers that had defined their lives and ruined the lives of others, could attack you for any random cause. It could be for slights real or imagined, or for the betrayal of one of the patchworks of behavioral standards in prison that did not come naturally to a man from privileged circles, like Mark.

While in El Dorado, Mark was assigned to kitchen detail, which meant his classification was, as he expected, going well. Mark had a lifelong interest in baking, but he had no experience baking chocolate-chip cookies on such a large scale. A small population of qualified inmates worked kitchen detail, leaving their cells early in the morning to work and coming back when others were out on less glamorous detail, such as mopping the hallways in an endless loop, a Sisyphean task performed as industrial-strength cleanser stripped out your nostrils.

As glad as Mark was to get kitchen detail, nothing in maximum security was simple. He was one of several given a key to a room storing flour and sugar. Once, he was threatened by a large, muscular inmate to give up the key, but he refused. Later, when bags were stolen, the man was blamed for the crime, and he thought Mark was the one who had turned him in.

One day, while Mark was talking on the pay phone to his father, the man approached him.

"What's up?"

Mark looked at him. "I'm on the phone," he said.

The man leaned in closer. "I said, 'what's up?'"

Mark had few options. He could fight the man to a double loss—he would get written up for fighting, imperiling his classification and case for parole, and he would lose the fight. Mark started talking, ultimately convincing the man that someone else had turned him in (Kristina maintains Mark did not turn snitch). Mark later joked that he had used every ounce of his business negotiation skills to get out of that situation.

El Dorado was a good place for Mark to find his footing. He had regular weekend visits from Kristina. Eric, who was one year old, was too young to know what was happening. Charlotte, who was four, happily played with her sticker books on the flight to Kansas and in the jail's visiting area. While Kristina was disappointed that Charlotte did not rush to her father's arms the first time she saw him in weeks, it was hard not to feel her heartstrings pulled when, as they were ready to leave, Charlotte asked if "Daddy could please pretty please" just walk her to the car.

Within a month, Mark was transferred to Lansing, the oldest prison in the state and the one where, early one morning, Dick Hickock and Perry Smith were dangled off the end of a rope until their feet tilted downward in the highest form of Kansas justice. Lansing had changed since the *In Cold Blood* killers had been hung there. Its name had been changed from the Kansas State Penitentiary to the Lansing Correctional Facility, with a majority of its facilities dedicated to medium and minimum security wings. Mark was assigned to live in a medium security dormitory that resembled a military barrack instead of a prison. The only downside was that, because of greater television privileges, more prisoners were aware of his case and standing. He was warned to expect the extortion attempts he had skirted in maximum security, but bluffed his way out of tense situations by claiming he had spent every last cent on his defense. His fellow inmates had more to lose than those in maximum and thus were less likely to risk a physical confrontation. Mark was thankful that he was still a convincing man.

The ruse about having nothing but lint in his pockets worked for Mark. In truth, because he had spared himself the exorbitant costs involved with a trial, Mark had a large amount of savings and stock options left from his high-salaried jobs. Kristina, with her affluent background and six-figure salary, likewise helped. She bought a home in Lansing, only a half hour from the Kansas City airport, and established regular weekend visits as part of a family routine. A later official prison photo of Mark showed him more at ease, having grown a goatee. That look of puzzled fear was gone.

In January, 2007, barely more than six months after pleading guilty, Mark was transferred to the minimum security wing at Lansing. This meant he had the privilege to work outside the facility, quite a coup for a convicted murderer only halfway through the first year of his sentence. These were labor-intensive work details for most—essentially chainless chain gangs—yet fate smiled on Mark again when he earned a plum assignment working in private industry.

Mark worked "off campus" at a firm called Impact Design. The company designed and manufactured clothing, such as shirts and hats, and earned tax advantages for putting inmates to work. Five percent of Mark's wages were garnered by a fund to benefit crime victims, though in something of a financial irony, ten percent was held for the benefit of Mark's own retirement, an assurance against inmates dying in destitution. At first, Mark performed menial tasks, but he increasingly took on a greater role advising management. Before long, the company started securing accounts from businesses like Tricots St. Raphael, owned by Perry Ellis. Management couldn't believe a Harvard MBA had fallen into their laps from behind the prison walls, though by that time Mark did not technically live behind a wall.

When Impact decided to move to Johnson County, of all places, Mark was forced to resign, since a prisoner could not work for a firm headquartered in the county in which he had committed his crime. It was a setback, but those who knew Mark had little doubt that he would regain his footing.

By this time, a third photo of Mark had been taken by the Kansas prison system. It showed a man comfortable in his own skin and surroundings. Looking like a veteran of the penal system, Mark had a close-shaved head and glasses. Stretching his neck up, Mark was back to his customary position of looking out, and looking ahead—no longer a man scared of what might be lurking behind him. And why not? In front of him lay the probability of an affluent future in a fancy suburb with a loving, supportive family. He is eligible for release on May 7, 2011.

* * * *

After giving out the protest fliers the day of the sentencings, John Harmon made a last visit to David's grave in Oak Lawn Cemetery in Olathe. He had gone two decades without seeing it and probably would never see it again. The distance between Chili and Olathe was too great. A church member had at one point offered to finance a move of David's body to Chili, but John said David had lived his life "right with the Sweet Jesus," and it was better to let him end his journey where he was. John understood why David had moved to Olathe to begin a new life.

The city had been changed inexorably thanks to that cascade of evangelicals David had been fortunate—and unlucky enough—to be part of. Olathe was, with George W. Bush in the White House, right at the center of the ascendancy of a conservative Christian America. This was what David had been promised when he was packing his bags to leave Chili.

The displacement of those lonely farmers in a fledgling Olathe was a distant memory. Farmers Insurance and Honeywell call Olathe home, along with dozens of companies that dot the numerous corporate and industrial parks in the city. In 2008, *Money* magazine ranked Olathe as the eleventh best place to live in America, up two notches from 2006, with a staggeringly low three-personal-crime incidents per every one thousand inhabitants, one of the lowest in the nation.

The spire of the College Church of the Nazarene still pierces the sky more noticeably than anything else around it. MidAmerica Nazarene College, not a generation old when Mark and Melinda first shared whispers in the dean's office, was now called MidAmerica Nazarene

University, with fewer restrictions these days, drawing great minds not only from across America but around the world. New buildings had sprung up like wildflowers, and the student body had increased almost tenfold since its inception. Sante Fe, the main drag and the well-marked former stagecoach trail where missionaries, trappers, traders, prospectors, and hustlers of every stripe had walked, was now a modern thoroughfare with a Chuck E. Cheese, a Starbucks, and one of the city's two Wal-Marts.

So wholesale was the change that there was no longer any discernable tension between the evangelicals and those old-time farming families. The housing stock had improved since then, quite markedly, with cul-de-sac upon cul-de-sac laid out with perfect geometric certitude, without the architectural and landscaping challenge of hills. Olathe, it was now said, was not named for the Shawnee Indian word "beautiful" or "duplex," but "another new evangelical church on the corner."

Like Melinda, Mark Mangelsdorf will one day soon leave Kansas for a second time. And for a second time, he will likely return to the higher echelons of society as a perfected soul who has paid for his crime and who is at peace with his God. In this cold-blooded business, one errant act, even one as brutal as the murder of David Harmon, does not have to define a life.

Acknowledgments

My debts of gratitude run varied and deep, and any listing will invariably leave some out, but here goes:

Thanks to Albert LaFarge, the best agent since the earth cooled, for endless guidance and the occasional free breakfast. Thanks also goes to many at Skyhorse Publishing including Tony Lyons, Brando Skyhorse, Lilly Golden, Alaina Sudeith, Erik Kennedy, and the entire team.

So many people related to the case, named and unnamed, quoted and anonymous, offered invaluable help by opening doors—both literal and figurative—to this painful and highly contentious case. Historical societies in both Olathe and Chili deserve special thanks, as do organizations from the Olathe Police Department, the Johnson County District Attorney's Office, the Office of the Attorney General for the State of Kansas, MidAmerica Nazarene University, the College Church of the Nazarene, and too many individuals to name though Joy Hempy, who bakes the best chocolate chip cookies in Kansas, must be noted. Endless credit also goes to fellow firefighters at Engine 46 for providing a good place to write and more. Readers: check the batteries on your smoke alarms tonight.